MW01092862

My Mastery:
Continued Education Through Jiu Jitsu

By Chris Matakas

My Mastery: Continued Education Through Jiu Jitsu
Copyright: Chris Matakas
Front Cover Photo by Eric Talerico Photography
Back Cover Photo by Bella Dreams Photography
Design by Mark Brehaut
Editing by Kathy Matakas
Published: June 30, 2015

BUILD THE FIRE
Publishing

Table of Contents

"We have not wings, we cannot soar;
But we have feet to scale and climb
By slow degrees, by more and more,
The cloudy summits of our time.

The mighty pyramids of stone
That wedge-like cleave the desert airs,
When nearer seen, and better known,
Are but gigantic flights of stairs."

-From The Ladder of St. Augustine by Henry
Wadsworth Longfellow

For the Purple Circle

Forward

> *If the ax is dull*
> *and its edge unsharpened,*
> *more strength is needed,*
> *but skill will bring success.*

Ecclesiastes 10:10

The proverbial ax can be a tool for violent resolution as well as ingenious creation. Jiu Jitsu is based on principles of efficiency and leverage--create maximum output with minimum input. In a world where we are pulled in every which direction, and when we grasp for help the answer more often than not is "just try harder." Chris Matakas teaches us to use Jiu Jitsu as a vehicle for creating balance and purpose in our lives.

I fell in love with Jiu Jitsu as a 15 year old boy, the day I first walked on to the mats at Gracie Barra, located in a suburb of Rio de Janeiro in 1992. My father wanted me to learn self-defense, but Jiu Jitsu gave me far more than that. It changed my life. Jiu Jitsu gave me direction and boundaries at an age I so desperately needed. Before I knew it I was winning National Championships, and in 1997 Master Renzo Gracie invited me to move to New York where I got to train under his personal guidance and teach at the Renzo Gracie Academy.

Through Jiu Jitsu I have lived a privileged life. Visited many countries and got to experience so many cultures.

Competed at the highest level having the chance to fight at the old Pride FC and the UFC Ultimate Fighting Championship. After retiring from competition I became a Mixed Martial Arts judge for the New Jersey State Athletic Control Board. As I write this foreward I am getting ready to pack my bags to go corner my student Frankie Edgar in the first UFC in the Phillipines. However, my greatest joy has always been and still is sharing my experiences on the mats with our students at our RABJJ Academy in Robbinsville, NJ and our second location in Newtown, PA where Coach Chris Matakas is the main instructor.

In 2008, Chris Matakas walked in to my school (back then in Hamilton, NJ) as a young college graduate. Very quickly his intelligence and physical ability allowed him to become a standout student. Chris was always very inquisitive on the mats but what struck me the most about him is that he was also looking for answers in his personal life.

One day Chris walked into the academy and told me he had removed the TV from his room, and that all he had was a bed and a stack of books. I immediately thought, "Why does this kid want to live as if he was in jail?" I later realized that it was the other way around. He was shielding himself from distractions, he was preparing to sharpen the ax and begin removing the nonessential. I believe it was in that moment where Chris took action on his search for meaning that this book was conceived.

The lessons in this book are less about success and more about purpose and direction. Jiu Jitsu as the proverbial ax used as a personal tool to create the life you always wanted to live but didn't know how. We want more but in fact we need less, get ready to sharpen the ax and hack away.

Jiu Jitsu Way of Life.

Ricardo Almeida
May 2015

Preface

With the overwhelmingly positive reception of my first book *My Mastery: Learning to Live Through Jiu Jitsu*, I felt it necessary to continue this journey together. Jiu Jitsu has become such a major aspect of my experience, and I have devoted a great deal of my waking hours to its understanding. As I mature, I find I am equally (if not more so) concerned with the growth of those around me in this art as I am my own. I love Jiu Jitsu, but even more so I love my fellow man. Every day I thank my lucky stars that I am afforded the opportunity to serve others through such a sacred medium.

At a certain point in one's training, he or she finds that they have on the most basic level, learned most of the techniques in the Jiu Jitsu practitioner's repertoire. True mastery, it turns out, is not found in accumulating each and every tool under the sun. True mastery is learning that there are really only a handful of tools, and it is the proper application with correct timing and setting that makes them so useful. In my own training from around Brown Belt on, I have found that the greatest gains in my ability to perform this art are not techniques, but concepts. Simple paradigm shifts that have an underlying unity in all positions. Mastery is a movement from the complex to the simple to the near invisible. The further I go into this art, the less it feels I am actually doing in its performance.

I wanted to continue this journey together, and I

thought the only means to best serve you, the student, is a practical application of philosophy in the art of grappling. *My Mastery* served as a great foundation in showing that there is more to Jiu Jitsu than armbars and berimbolos. We discussed the ultimate goal of Jiu Jitsu not in mastery of chokes, but in mastery of self. It is my goal with this text to further this study. I believe this book will serve all readers well, but if the original *My Mastery* was for the beginner or general student, this edition in our series will be more aptly used by the contemplative seeker who recognizes Jiu Jitsu as the vehicle that it is. The growth of the Jiu Jitsu community has seemingly adopted this "Jiu Jitsu way of life," but this is only the beginning. Now, we collectively turn our attention toward what this mode of living entails and the highest ideals that make it a reality.

In the following pages, I have put forth the most fundamental thought paradigms that have best served my goal of achieving whatever degree of technical mastery my circumstance allows. As with the first book, each of these topics translates off that mat into day-to-day experience. For the sincere student, it mustn't be enough to simply understand Jiu Jitsu. We must seek to understand ourselves! I believe Jiu Jitsu, at least for our community, is the best means of doing so.

As the title suggests, I consider this book a continuation of the first. It is my hope that it will help the reader reach new heights in both Jiu Jitsu and in life. These books can be read in a series or independently, for I believe that which you study is only matched in importance by the sincerity with which you approach it. The fact that you have devoted a portion of your life to reading this book amid a world of flashing lights and blinking screens proves that you are sincere in your pursuit, and your success in this endeavor is assured.

This book is conceptual and philosophical in nature. It will not teach you how to do an armbar. It will, however, teach you why to do an armbar, what makes an armbar possible, and how we can use armbars to learn more about ourselves and the world in which we live, all the while never mentioning arm bars. My study of this art, from white belt to black, has given me more in the ways of personal growth and self-understanding than I had ever expected. Without a doubt, my commitment to Jiu Jitsu has been the most fruitful endeavor of my life.

I applaud you on your journey, and wish you all the best. As we began *My Mastery*, so shall we begin this text, with a reinforcing of our purpose guiding this endeavor:

Jiu Jitsu is the vehicle. Not the Road.

Chris Matakas
Hamilton, NJ
May 2015

The Ax

One needn't read more than a page of my writing to learn my affinity for quotes. Words make the intangible aspects of human experience communicable, and a single sentence can shatter our world view and assist us in the formulation of a new one. Quotes help us see what the great men of the past saw and feel what they felt. They bridge the gap of time and connect us with men long past in our shared experience of being human. Quotes are awesome. Quotes tell a story. A stringing together of a few words can leave you with an idea that changes the course of your life and directs you toward reaching your highest potential as a human. The story they tell is derived from the experience which inspired them, and it is our sharing that experience that allows for the quote to resonate so deeply within our being.

It seems nearly half of what I say is a quote from some bard or sage, and I would speak only in the words of the great men of old had I had less respect for my own life. Thoreau and Huxley calmly state what I have spent years trying to articulate and never found the words for doing so. To read the words of these great men is to read the highest expression of my very self which is inexpressible due to the shortcomings of my particular nature. This is so, undoubtedly, but I must forge ahead in folly with my own feeble attempts of communicating to the world what I believe, in my own words.

Life is not without irony as I will attempt to do this through a metaphor that I myself did not create, and odds are probably neither did he who is quoted. I chose this quote for a multitude of reasons, and the story behind its placement in this text is one I deem worthy of sharing.

Outside of my love of others and love for my own existence, I have no greater love than that of nature. I have always been pulled to the simplicity of the woods, and have found comparable fellowship among trees to that of man. I love man, and I have been fortunate enough to know many great ones, but nothing has ever moved me or inspired me more than mother nature herself. There is a calmness, and definitive purpose in nature that I have never found expressed in society. A connection with the universal energy far greater than myself has always been visible among the trees in a way the modern achievements could never express. I seek counsel with the woods practically daily, and whenever I feel as though I have lost my path, an afternoon walk through nature always brings me back. Only one man-made object has ever moved me in a way such as nature, and that was the Lincoln Memorial in Washington, D.C.

I was blessed to have experienced this monument with two dear friends and fellow Ricardo Almeida black belts, Maximillian Bohanon and Peter McHugh. It is their fellowship that made this testament to a great life all the more enjoyable. I stood in awe at this cenotaph, and his words engraved on either side pierced my soul. A man, a man just like me, lived his life in a way that was deserving of such acknowledgment. This moved me beyond words. I was paralyzed with awe. Not for the acknowledgment itself but what this acknowledge represents.

Abraham Lincoln stood for something, fought for something, and forever changed the world and lives of all of those in it. This was a great man, but he was still a man. I instantly knew the course my life would take. Though I will probably never affect the world to the degree that he did, it would not be for lack of trying. Every opportunity with another was an opportunity to serve my fellow man. Every moment alone was a chance to grow and become more of who I already was. I instantly felt how great a life could be and that this was only made possible by service toward others.

In the words of Thoreau, "I am confined by the narrowness of my experience." I may not have the opportunity to serve all of America like Honest Abe did, but I do have the opportunity to serve those within my circle of influence, and my writing has become a big part of this service. This text is an expression of that service, and one which I thought best outlined by perhaps the most quoted phrase by this great man:

"Give me six hours to chop down a tree, and I will spend the first four sharpening the ax."

This quote has always rung true deep within my mind. I have always derived a sense of self as someone who may not be the most talented or the brightest, but given enough time, I can do or figure out anything. My greatest gift has been my ability to sit alone in the woods or at a keyboard and sharpen my ax. In fact, as I age I find the sharpening of the ax even more enjoyable than the swinging of it.

The wisdom expressed in this quote deemed worthy of further explanation, and so this text will attempt to follow its wisdom and its application in Jiu Jitsu and subsequently, life.

In keeping with this theme, this book has been broken down into four sections: Understanding the Ax, Sharpening the Ax, Swinging the Ax, and Putting the Ax down. The ax serves as a perfect metaphor for Jiu Jitsu. A vehicle with which we carve the tangible and intangible of daily life. We must understand Jiu Jitsu, cultivate the ability to learn and practice with sincere purpose, and then take what we have learned and apply these lessons to the totality of our being.

Ultimately, we must put the ax down, but only after we have carved away all of the inessential of our being as we ascend toward a more actualized life. After all, it was never really the tree we were chopping down, but ourselves.

Part I - Understanding the Ax

"A musician must make music, an artist must paint, a poet must write, if he is to be ultimately at peace with himself. What a man can be, he must be."-Abraham Maslow

Begin With End In Mind

"Where there is no vision, people perish."-
Proverbs 29:18

I have been fortunate to have had the time and desire to read many books in my life. The vast majority of which have been in the realm of philosophy and self-improvement. I find myself constantly referencing a handful of books over the years, and Stephen Covey's *The 7 Habits of Highly Effective People* is one of the most common. I strongly, strongly recommend you read this book if you have not already, and if you have, read it again. After all, you are not the same person you were when you read it! Understanding these seven habits has helped guide my life, but Habit #2- Begin with the End in Mind has done so more than any other. So much so in fact, that I find myself subconsciously asking this question throughout the day for the most menial of tasks.

Begin with the end in mind.

This is so abstract and yet poignant at the same time, that when asked for advice I find myself always giving some variation of this idea as a response. We must know where we want to go in order to get there. Our modern lives are growing increasingly chaotic, and it is only a clear, definitive purpose that will keep us on track. If you do not know where you want to go, you will probably never get there. I'm reminded of the wisdom from Lewis Carroll's *Alice in Wonderland*:

> *"Would you tell me, please, which way I ought to go from here?"*
> *"That depends a good deal on where you want to get to," said the Cat.*
> *"I don't much care where—" said Alice.*
> *"Then it doesn't matter which way you go," said the Cat.*

In understanding this truth, it is no longer enough simply to put forth effort in our endeavors. We must know where we want to go, and apply specific effort toward a concentrated aim. On the whole, a Jiu Jitsu practitioner must understand why they are training Jiu Jitsu in the first place. What are your goals?

Do you train because you want to compete? To fight? Do you train because you want to lose weight? Become more confident? Have a great workout? Do you train as a vehicle for learning? Do you train to find fellowship?

Clearly, these goals vary greatly and the resulting steps taken by these various minded practitioners will not be the same. Consider a 20-something male who wants to fight MMA vs. a 40-something mom who wants to lose weight. These students will operate in two very different paradigms and their resulting training should be equally different. In knowing where you want to go, and beginning with this end in mind, you can better plot the course ahead to most efficiently meet your goals.

The same holds true for small scale daily operations. We show up to training each day with our own preconceived reasons for doing so, and the better we understand these reasons the higher likelihood of having those desires met. If I am a serious student focusing on technical growth, I'd better have a clear goal for the training session. I should pick one or two techniques or ideas, and seek out those areas in training as often as possible. I try to always have a clear focus for a type of guard I want to play, a type of guard pass I want to work, and a submission. That way, no matter where the roll goes, I am always in a position to work on an aspect of my game that I have previously determined necessary. This is the sole focus of my training, and my training resembles this.

Were I training Jiu Jitsu for MMA, my training would consist of very different focuses. Maybe I'd focus on getting up off my back when on bottom, and settling in half guard for ground and pound on top. Again, this is very different than the sport Jiu Jitsu focus. If I am a student of learning focusing on the concept of efficiency, my movements will be small and precise, and I will use as little of my physical faculties as possible. If my goal is weight loss, then I would be training at the highest pace possible, constantly keeping my heart rate elevated. In a sense, I would be as inefficient as possible.

It becomes most apparent that the goal of the

practitioner greatly determines the way in which he or she trains, and we soon realize the importance of knowing what that goal is. Understanding where we want to go is the first step in getting there. This must precede all action in order to ensure that action is properly directed. In doing so, you can be sure that you will make the most of your time, and move on the clearest path toward your goal.

Begin with the end in mind, and you will achieve the end you had in mind!

Purpose

"Let no act be done without purpose."- Marcus Aurelius

Those who develop great skill in Jiu Jitsu, or anything for that matter, are those who have made a conscious choice to do so. It is not enough to simply show up and train hard. We must train with a clearly defined purpose, and have a heading toward which we set our course. The more clearly we determine our goals the more achievable they become. In the first *My Mastery*, I talked about the importance of specificity in training. I showed that my areas of focus in training were five-fold:

An open (distance) guard pass and sweep.
An close (compact) guard pass and sweep.
A submission.

This way, regardless of whether I was on top or bottom, close or far, or in an advantageous position such as side control or the mount, I was always in a position to improve upon a skill of my choosing. This is extremely specific, and serves as simply an example of training in a purposeful way. It is for each of us to determine the best mode of purposeful practice for ourselves, and to act accordingly.

Lately, I find myself focusing on more generalized themes. The approach has changed, but the strength of purpose remains the same. Whether the focus is smash passing on top, or leg locks on bottom, I am going in to every training session with a clearly defined goal. This clarity ensures that I will make the most of my training session, and that it will serve to push me toward building the skills that I have consciously decided my game requires. Jiu Jitsu is the most enjoyable activity I have undertaken, and I train daily with friends I dearly love. It becomes very easy to get lost in the moment, and a two-hour training session passes in the blink of an eye. Yes, we trained hard. Yes, we breathed heavy. Yes, we certainly got better.

But did we get better in those areas that we had prioritized with a clear head? This is what matters.

I thoroughly enjoy the works of the Stoics of Ancient Greece. They talk simply about the shortness of life, and the urgency with which we live. Seneca said it best in his first letter to Lucilius,

"Therefore, Lucilius, do as you write me that you are doing: hold every hour in your grasp. Lay hold of to-day's task, and you will not need to depend so much upon to-morrow's. While we are postponing, life speeds by. Nothing, Lucilius, is ours, except time. We were entrusted by nature with the ownership of this single thing, so fleeting and slippery that anyone who will can oust us from possession. What fools these mortals be! They allow the cheapest and most useless things, which can easily be replaced, to be charged in the reckoning, after they have acquired them; but they

never regard themselves as in debt when they have received some of that precious commodity, – time! And yet time is the one loan which even a grateful recipient cannot repay."

This holds true for our Jiu Jitsu lives as well. We will only have so many training sessions in our lives. Whether due to injuries, obligations, or the like, each training session is one more closer to our last. We owe it to ourselves to be sure that we make the most of each one. Mastery lies on an infinite continuum, and as a result we will never reach the end. We can, however, see to it that we are as far along that continuum as our circumstance allows. This is only made possible by clearly defined goals, and training with great purpose in pursuit of these goals.

Train with purpose, and strive toward whatever potential your existence allows.

Values

*"First say to yourself what you would be; and then do what you have to do."-Epictetu*s

This is perhaps the easiest advice to give, and yet the hardest to truly receive. If I could give only one piece of advice to someone beginning a life of personal development it would be simply to know your values. This is the knowledge that must precede all action. We must remember that all actions are preceded by thought, and it is the thoughts themselves that take manifest in the form of actions. Properly directed thoughts result in properly directed actions. The only way to appropriately guide our thoughts is to know their foundation, our values.

This is the beginning of self-awareness, and it is self-awareness which is the beginning of the end of suffering and the bedrock on which a life of meaning is built. When we know our values, we can easily measure whether or not our actions are in accordance with them. Values are the measuring sticks with which we determine the worthiness of our actions. To be better associated with one's own values is to remove a lot of the needless activities of daily life.

Albert Einstein used to wear the same clothes every day to avoid wasting precious time and mental energy dressing himself. This is a man who knew his values, and recognized he was spending a portion of his life each day acting contrary to them, and so he removed this inefficiency. Henry David Thoreau went to the woods because he "wished to live deliberately." Epicurus, the great philosopher from ancient Greece, lived off bread and olives with the occasional bite of cheese to avoid excess in the pursuit of a higher existence. Isaac Newton was a recluse and spent much of his time in solitary study. Prince Siddhartha Gautama gave up a kingdom of wealth in pursuit of the life of an ascetic on his way to becoming the Buddha.

All these men recognized what they themselves valued, and lived according to these values regardless of their relationship to the values of their community. Each lived according to what brought them happiness and peace rather than commonplace prescriptions of the multitudes. I have spent a great deal of time studying how great men of the past defined success, and John Wooden and Earl Nightingale hit the nail on the head.

"Success is the peace of mind attained through the self satisfaction of knowing you made the effort to do the best of which you are capable."- John Wooden

"Success is the progressive realization of a worthy ideal."- Earl Nightingale

What do these two definitions have in common? They define success as a personally defined subjective term. Ourselves, and only ourselves, have the ability to define and measure success for ourselves. No one can do this for us. Consider John Wooden's definition. He defines success as the peace of mind (subjective), referencing *self*-satisfaction regarding the best of which *you* are capable. This is a personal relationship between our values and our efforts. Consider Earl Nightingale's definition. A "worthy ideal" can only be considered worthy to the individual if it aligns with his or her values.

Only we can determine if we are successful, and it is only when our actions run parallel with our values that this becomes a reality. To know our values is to have a foundation on which to build a great life. Our environment and education will play a large part in influencing our formulation of this world view, but is ultimately ourselves that have the final say. We must decide what we value, and then live accordingly. After all, in the eyes of the world we could achieve great success, but if our actions do not coincide with what we ourselves truly deem worthy, we will find no peace.

Know your values, and you will know yourself. It is then that we find our success.

Four Levels of Skill

"We have learned a lot, Siddhartha, there is still much to learn. We are not going around in circles, we are moving up, the circle is a spiral, we have already ascended many a level."- Govinda from Hermann Hesse's Siddhartha

As an instructor I find myself answering the same few questions, albeit in different forms, throughout the years. One of the most common concerns I hear, especially from the more experienced student, is:

"I am getting worse. What am I doing wrong?"

We all have felt this way at one time or another. We ride the crests and troughs of knowledge acquisition, and without fail our highs are followed by a low. In the circular nature of skill development, we must always come around again. I am quick to remind our concerned student that they are not getting worse, no matter what feedback they believe their training to be giving them. They are, however, becoming aware of their shortcomings that once went unnoticed. This is a painful but absolute necessity for the evolving practitioner as awareness always precedes growth.

There are four levels of skill. No more, no less. Each of us lies along this continuum in every area of life, and in understanding our position we are afforded the opportunity to improve it.

The Four Levels of Skill:

1. *Unconsciously Bad* - You stink, and you don't know you stink.

2. *Consciously Bad* - You stink, and you know you stink (Where we find our above mentioned student).

...The turning point toward the heights!

3. *Consciously Good* - You are competent, dare we say skilled, but only with the focus of conscious attention. Essentially, you consistently remind yourself to perform the right actions.

4. *Unconsciously Good* - The holy grail. You are good, and you no longer have to think about it. You perform your actions instinctively, and there is no need for conscious thought.

No matter the skill, your growth will follow this trajectory. Now we can clearly see that when we feel down because we are "getting worse," we have actually ascended to the next level of skill acquisition. Is it painful? Sure. But it is this frustration that fuels us to not sit contently in the second tier, and strive to bridge the gap from incompetent to competent.

A final thought on this topic.

It is worth noting that each of us lies along varying degrees of this continuum in various areas of Jiu Jitsu. You may be a "4" in guard passing, and the bee's knees of your academy, all the while being a "2" in guard play. This holds true for all Jiu Jitsu practitioners, including the world champions. Even the best in the world are "1s" and "2s" in certain aspects of Jiu Jitsu. They simply are skilled enough to not allow their opponent to bring them into that arena.

When we honestly take stock of our ability, we are then granted the opportunity to improve our circumstance. Accessing where you stand is the only way to stand somewhere else. The most challenging aspect of this experience is to bridge the gap from being 1- Unconsciously Bad to 2- Consciously Bad. After all, if we stink but don't know we stink, how can we expect to change that? This is where we must make honest assessment of ourselves, and seek opinions from peers and instructors we respect. Once you make it to Level #2, Level #4 is within your capacity with enough purposely directed attention.

Determine where you are, and move onward!

Level Playing Field

"People are always blaming circumstances for what they are. I don't believe in circumstances. The people who get on in this world are the people who get up and look for the circumstances they want, and, if they can't find them, make them."- George Bernard Shaw

To be fair, this chapter's title is misleading. Nowhere in human activity does there exist a level playing field. We all have different genetic makeups and histories, each of which combine to leave all of us with certain predispositions toward success in various fields of human achievement. Having said this, I believe Jiu Jitsu more than any other activity negates many of these imbalances between men.

Jiu Jitsu is infinite, and requires no particularly skilled practitioner in order to excel. Just look across your mats, or watch any tournament. We have men, women. Some tall, some short. Strong and bulky, small and fast. The body types are endless, and yet all find success in their own way. It is the limitless variables of grappling which make this possible. A small, flexible practitioner may find affinity in flashy, spinning techniques like the berimbolo. A broader, stockier player will find great comfort in performing under the leg guard passes, using his size as an advantage. There is no concrete way to play Jiu Jitsu, and this is why so many different types of people find joy in it. We can all be highly skilled, and we can do so in ways which vary as much as our appearances.

All traditional sports, field sports specifically, have greatly reduced styles of game play. Take football for example. There are only so many ways to play this game, and they all involve the player being big, fast, strong, and athletic. If you want to play quarterback in the NFL, its an almost prerequisite to be 6'5". If you want to play wide receiver, you better run a 40-yard dash creeping toward the 4-second mark. If you want to play lineman, well you need to be 300 pounds or so, while being extremely agile.

We just excluded the vast majority of humanity. All of the most popularized sports have over the years required a more and more specialized athlete in order to succeed. This is why the average person is becoming farther and farther removed from being able to compete on this level. But Jiu Jitsu is different. Big guys can play big guy games. Small guys can play small guy games. Flexible play the flexible. Strong play the strong. The fast play fast. The infinitude of Jiu Jitsu allows for the infinitude of the types of practitioners. There exists a game for each and every one of us which is specifically possible within the confines of our particular skill set.

Jiu Jitsu gives each of us something that no other sport can. We have the opportunity to become truly great regardless of what circumstance fate has handed us. We have complete freedom and responsibility to achieve whatever level of mastery we wish.

Can we really ask for anything more?

Don't Compare Yourself To Others

"Do what you can, with what you have, where you are."- Theodore Roosevelt

This is a topic that I find myself addressing time after time. I mentioned it in the first *My Mastery*, and in a few blog posts, but this will continue to bear repeating until we learn the lesson as it holds true in all areas of life. Perhaps the greatest disservice you can pay yourself is to compare yourself to others, and this holds true for a plethora of reasons.

There has never been a you before.

In the history of history, there has never been someone with your particular genetic make-up or life experiences. This being the case, we have no reference points with which to compare ourselves, and therefore it is futile to attempt to measure yourself relative to others. We can gauge no sense of self-worth external to ourselves. This is a fool's errand, folly by many and holds equally true regarding Jiu Jitsu.

We each have different body types and athletic abilities which leave us predisposed to competency or inadequacy in various aspects of grappling. We each have different mental faculties which allow for varying degrees of conscious understanding of concepts and techniques. We each have learned from different instructors who bring their own biases into their teaching of Jiu Jitsu. We each have different goals regarding our training, and thus approach grappling in very different ways. We lead such different lives that greatly affect the time that we are afforded to devote to this study. For these reasons and many more, it is absolutely ridiculous to compare yourself to others. This will get you nowhere as you'll spend your time focusing on that which you cannot control, others, versus that which you can control, yourself.

The best yardstick for our progress is not other people, but ourselves. Am I better than I was yesterday? This is the only question worth asking. As long as you go to bed at night a better practitioner than the one who woke up that morning, you have succeeded. Your worth should have nothing to do with how your progress stacks up relative to another. My dear friend Leandro Hernandez, Ricardo Almeida Brown Belt Instructor, once told me that if you get 1% better each day, in 3 months (about 100 days) you will be twice as good as you are today. That way of thinking is simple and profound.

Consider the compound effect we so often hear about regarding investing. If you invest a one-time sum of $10,000, and the market returns annually at 8%, you are closing in on half a million dollars in 50 years. The financial elite know this, and use it wisely. Einstein said, "The most powerful force in the universe is compound interest." The same holds true for education! Every day we build upon our knowledge base, and that knowledge continues to compound upon itself.

By focusing on your progress in a vacuum, regardless of how it compares to others, you will achieve great heights without the associated frustration of competing against others. After all, we are not competing against others in anything. Not in Jiu Jitsu, finances, or worldly achievements. When we are on our death beds, we will not say, "You know, I'm glad my guard passing was better than so-and-so." Or "Man, I'm glad my Roth IRA is bigger than that dude's." We will only be concerned with how we did in this life, relative to how we potentially could have done.

Michael Jordan said that the reason he had the success he did on the basketball court was his standards. He had higher standards for himself than anyone. Everyone was busy trying to compete with him while he was competing with who he had the potential to be. That difference, is the reason why he is Michael Jordan.

We must be as diligent in our standards, and our measuring stick must be ourselves.

Am I better than I was yesterday? Did I put forth my maximum effort? Did I truly try?

These are the only questions worth asking regarding our progress in this art. Am I on the way to achieving my potential as a practitioner of this art? My potential, not the perceived potential of another. When we do this in Jiu Jitsu, it is our responsibility as an evolving member of the human race to do this in all areas of life.

Then we will truly succeed.

Jiu Jitsu is the Vehicle

"Many men fish all their lives without ever realizing that it is not fish they are after."-Unknown

Jiu Jitsu is the vehicle. Not the road.

This is the best description I have yet to come up with for my relationship to Jiu Jitsu. This sentence is how I began and ended the first *My Mastery*, and for good reason. Marcus Aurelius once said, "Strive to be the man philosophy wished to make you." He could have just as easily been talking about Jiu Jitsu. This is the vehicle that allows us to navigate the road of life. Whatever your goal is, Jiu Jitsu will facilitate it.

Consider all of the efforts and hours you have put into your Jiu Jitsu training. All of the sweat and pulled muscles. This cannot be just for Jiu Jitsu in and of itself. It has to be for something more. Yes, you have been molding your ability to perform Jiu Jitsu for all these years, but you have been more importantly molding who you are as a person. Jiu Jitsu is the sculptor, and you are the clay. It is with this art that we strive and reach for our highest ideals not as athletes, but as people.

I believe we must pursue mastery for who we become along the way in its achievement. When we progress in Jiu Jitsu, that newfound experience and wisdom transcends into all areas of our lives. We use Jiu Jitsu as the vehicle for growth, but that growth radiates over all of human activity. Someone who devotes time and energy in learning this skill is learning far more than how to subdue an opponent. The student learns persistence, perseverance, pattern recognition, problem solving, and most importantly, learning *how* to learn. In the arena of life, these virtues are far more valuable than any guard pass.

I believe the real reason we pursue anything in life is not for the thing itself, but for who we become on the way to its accomplishment. We strive to accomplish things in the attempt to mold ourselves. The greatest benefits Jiu Jitsu will have in your life will have nothing to do with Jiu Jitsu. It is this simple understanding that allows me to persist in my study. Even on the rare days when I may not have a burning desire to practice Jiu Jitsu, I am reminded that my practicing Jiu Jitsu is more accurately my practicing to become a better human being. The lessons I learn on the mat will serve me in every area of life-- personal development, relationships, business, and the like.

We strive to grow in Jiu Jitsu because we strive to grow in life. Jiu Jitsu is the vehicle that makes all personal development possible, and this road is a journey worth taking.

Socratic Ignorance

"What is the first business of one who practices philosophy? To get rid of self-conceit. For it is impossible for anyone to begin to learn that which he thinks he already knows."-Epictetus

One of the greatest obstacles to your growth in Jiu Jitsu will be your own knowledge, or more accurately, your perception of knowledge. As soon as we believe we understand something, we are immediately more resistant to entertaining new perspectives about that phenomenon. This concept will either be your greatest ally or your greatest fault. This paradigm has been discussed at length throughout history, and so we will use history to articulate its message.

Around 2,400 years ago in ancient Athens, mankind was dealt a humbling blow to our collective self-confidence, and it came by the way of Socrates.

We all know the name Socrates, but few know what he stood for. In my eyes his greatest lesson came when the Oracle at Delphi proclaimed Socrates to be the wisest man in all of Greece, and Socrates immediately sought to prove the Oracle wrong, for he knew how little he actually knew. He went on an inquisition, seeking in all the wise men of Athens a man who knew more than he. Time and time again, he came across men who claimed great knowledge over human affairs and man's deepest metaphysical questions. Time and time again, he was astonished at how little these "wise" men actually knew, and even more amazed at their inability to admit their ignorance. Ultimately, though full of self-doubt, Socrates accepted the Oracle's proclamation that he was the wisest of all men because *though he knew nothing, at least he knew that.*

This is the greatest lesson Socrates has bestowed upon us. One of the founders of Western Philosophy, and the apparent source of much of Plato's great work, Socrates is widely considered one of the greatest thinkers in human history. Whether it be Epistemology, Ethics or the Socratic Method, Socrates has handed down many tools with which each and every one of us navigates the world, and was the foundation for much of modern thought. This being said, he was open and honest about his own ignorance, and never claimed great knowledge over anything. This is worth holding onto.

One of the greatest minds to have ever lived proclaimed complete ignorance over the ways of the world.

This is described beautifully in Plato's *Meno* when *Meno* accuses Socrates of purposefully bewildering others and enchanting them with his words, perplexing all with whom he conversed. Socrates simply replies,

> *"For I perplex others, not because I am clear, but because I am utterly perplexed myself."*

It is this admittance of ignorance that is the starting point for all knowledge.

If one's mind is full of their perceived truths, and leaves no room for doubt or the entertaining of other possibilities, education and the associated acquisition of understanding die with it. This is the beginning of the end for man. It is only when we can admit our ignorance to ourselves and others that we leave room for real wisdom to take route.

In today's world, we have access to the totality of human knowledge in the palm of our hand, and we egoically mistake this knowledge as our own. We have labels and universally accepted descriptions of all phenomena, and we accept them as a matter of fact. But we must dig deeper. We must truly question.

We have not even come to an agreed upon definition of what knowledge actually is. Epistemologists have come to a loose description of knowledge as justified true belief which is not based off false assumptions, but even this is fallacious as the prerequisite knowledge required for justification makes this a circular definition.

So, if philosophers can't even agree upon a definition of knowledge, and if one of the greatest minds to have ever lived outwardly proclaimed, "The only thing I know is that I know nothing," I would say our own confidence in our understanding of the world (or Jiu Jitsu for that matter) is greatly unwarranted, and a hindrance to the elevation of man. If one sits quietly and entertains the question, "What do I know?" I am confident he will soon come to a place of complete naiveté. This is terrifying, humbling and at the same time inspiring. Here is a simple example of our misidentification with labels:

When we look up at the night sky, we see stars. We "know" they are stars, and leave it at that. Walk outside tonight, and once again look at that star, but don't call it a star. When we name something, we claim knowledge over it, and it is that name which gets in the way of our understanding of it. Look at that star again, and this time ask what it is. Not what it is called, but what is it? If you are not paralyzed by wonder, then you are missing one of the greatest aspects of the human experience.

Consider the words of English poet G.K. Chesterton vis a vis Alan Watts' *The Book: On The Taboo Against Knowing Who You Are*,

"It is a special kind of enlightenment to have this feeling that the usual, the way things normally are, is odd—uncanny and highly improbable. G. K. Chesterton once said that it is one thing to be amazed at a gorgon or a griffin, creatures which do not exist; but it is quite another and much higher thing to be amazed at a rhinoceros or a giraffe, creatures which do exist and look as if they don't."

The ability to doubt is a skill just like any other. Doubt

is the skill that leads to understanding. Doubt as much as you possibly can. Question everything, and then question some more. This is the starting point for one's education.

For one last time let's seek external council in the words of Isaac Newton,

"I do not know what I may appear to the world, but to myself I seem to have been only like a boy playing on the sea-shore, and diverting myself in now and then finding a smoother pebble or a prettier shell than ordinary, whilst the great ocean of truth lay all undiscovered before me."

Socrates. Isaac Newton. This is company worth keeping. If these great men claimed so little knowledge over their respective fields, how can we begin to claim any real knowledge over Jiu Jitsu? When we make allowance for our ignorance, and we properly define our relationship with Jiu Jitsu as such, we are afforded the opportunity to humbly study this art. It is only when we admit our ignorance that we can hope to overcome it.

Thought Exercise

Empty your Cup

One day, the great Zen master received a visit from his most renowned student. Though brilliant and worldly successful, this student was bound up by ego and full of pride.

The master served tea. He filled his student's cup to the brim, and then kept on pouring.

The student watched as the cup overflowed, making a mess all over the kitchen table. Finally, he could no longer restrain himself as he yelled, "The cup is full. No more will go in!"

Calmly the master set down the teapot.

"Like this cup," he said, "You are full of your own beliefs and opinions. How can I show you Zen unless you first empty your cup?"

We must ask ourselves who do we resemble: the master or the student. Are we holding on to previous beliefs and world views that are preventing us from attaining new heights? Are we truly open to other's teachings, or are we preoccupied with our own?

Part II - Sharpening the Ax

"We are at our very best, and we are happiest, when we are fully engaged in work we enjoy on the journey toward the goal we've established for ourselves. It gives meaning to our time off and comfort to our sleep. It makes everything else in life so wonderful, so worthwhile."-Earl Nightingale

Raise Your Standards

"Any time you sincerely want to make a change, the first thing you must do is to raise your standards."-Tony Robbins

I have spent a great deal of time since college studying personal development. Tony Robbins has had a tremendous impact on my life. I have read many of his books, and listened to just about every piece of audio media he has ever put out. I have learned many great lessons from this man, and perhaps the most impactful breakthrough on my life is his concept of "musts vs. shoulds."

Very simply, Tony often teaches that if you want to change your life, you must raise your standards. This is done by taking a look at your own psychology, and considering what are your "musts," the things we must do each day, versus what are our "shoulds," what we feel we should do each day. He teaches that people always meet their musts, but rarely meet their shoulds. Therefore, the simplest way to create change is to change your musts.

This is amazing advice for all areas of life, and is equally suitable to create lasting change regardless of the arena. We have talked about having a purpose for each training session. This purpose is acted upon by meeting your "musts" for the training session. Let's consider how raising your standards can improve your practicing of Jiu Jitsu.

Must vs. Shoulds:

> *I must learn a new technique this training session* vs. *I should learn a new technique this training session*
>
> *I must ask my teacher a question today* vs. *I should ask my teacher a question today*
>
> *I must help a less-experience student today* vs. *I should help a less-experienced student today*
>
> *I must work on this particular guard pass today* vs. *I should work on this particular guard pass today*

We very quickly see the difference between the two. If we took two students of similar skill, it would not take long to see the progress of our "must" student far surpass that of our "should" student.

This very simple paradigm shift makes the difference in who we become as practitioners and as people. If you are struggling in any area of life, it is simply because you are meeting your musts and not your shoulds. Raise your musts, and you will raise your quality of life.

If your income is a certain amount, then that is your

current standard for yourself. That is your must.

The way your body looks is a direct reflection of the standard you have for your body.

The love you experience in your relationships is a reflection of your interpersonal standards.

Your progress as a Jiu Jitsu practitioner is a *direct* reflection of the standards you have for yourself. If you see yourself as someone who is "OK" and progresses slowly, you will do just that. If you hold yourself to the standard of daily and relentlessly improving, and your must is to grow each day, you will meet that standard. This is simple, yet incredibly profound.

If you raise your musts, you will raise your quality of life. Define your musts and you define yourself.

Automaticity of Training

"The chains of habit are too weak to be felt until they are too strong to be broken."-Samuel Johnson

In the first *My Mastery* I stated, "Mastery, to whatever degree your circumstance allows, is determined by a handful of choices repeated daily." It has been two years since this book's release, and I stand by those words even more so today than when I wrote them. This is the very simple recipe to mastery, and it's why so few people achieve high levels of cognitive understanding or physical ability in any endeavor. This is the monotonous, simplistic truth that separates the progressing from the idle. Most people are capable of trying extremely hard in any given moment. Most people are capable of having great discipline for a short period of time. Most people are willing to make sacrifices today. Very few are willing to do these for years straight and even decades.

In our academy, morning sessions have been the baptism by fire as this is when the professionals and instructors get their main training in. If I had to wake up each day, and consciously think about what I am going to go through an hour from now, I would go back to bed. This especially held true during my brief MMA days, when I would spend my mornings sparring with MMA royalty. When you wake up cold and sore on a winter Tuesday morning in New Jersey, knowing that in one hour you will be getting punched in the face by a Ricardo Almeida or a Frankie Edgar, you very quickly learn to put your mornings on autopilot without much foresight for what's to come. I believe this is one of the greatest gifts we can have on the road to any meaningful competency of a skill.

We experience something known as "decision fatigue." This idea simply states that the more decisions we have to make, the harder it becomes to make the responsible choice as our will runs dry. The more we are able to remove decisions as our habits become automatic, the easier it becomes to consistently perform the right actions, and the more will we have to make the right decisions when it counts.

It is the cultivation of habits which removes the decision-making process.

Who we become is simply a reflection of our daily habits. As Tony Robbins has said, "Show me your habits and I'll show you who you'll become." The more we can automatize the essentials in our lives the more we will consistently grow. Every day, no matter what, the first thing I do after I put in my contacts in the morning is go downstairs and make a shake. This is an absolute must. I ensure that regardless of the rest of my day, I start out by fueling my body with water and nutrients. After that, Monday through Saturday mornings I either go to the gym or the academy to train. I *always* do something to improve my physical health. I then spend every afternoon reading or writing, as I am equally if not more concerned with my mental health as my physical health. This is always followed by an evening of service toward my students.

These are habits I cultivate. It is not fun drink kale shakes first thing in the morning. It is not easy to lift weights or train Jiu Jitsu. Reading challenging books is difficult, and sometimes writing doesn't come easy. Some days I feel I don't have the energy to be a good servant to others. But by making these actions which I do automatically, without the need for decisions or self-encouragement, I am able to live a life where these actions will compound over a lifetime into the man I will someday become. Just as important, by keeping my "decision well" full, I am able to make the proper choices when serving others. I have my complete capacity to do my best to love others as myself, and to try to follow the lead of the great men who came before me. We all have interactions with various individuals in our lives who drain us and test out mettle, but at least I am putting myself in the best position possible to be able to always make the right choices in their best interest.

Much of my life is spent in purposeful thought. I think this is one of the greatest gifts we have been given, but if we spend our whole lives in this state of attentiveness, we quickly break down. Wherever possible, determine which habits will best serve you and those around you, and cultivate the ability to make these actions automatic. The more we can automate the good, the stronger we will be to navigate the bad!

Simplicity

"In proportion as he simplifies his life, the laws of the universe will appear less complex."-Henry David Thoreau

Mastery is a movement from the complex to the simple. If you compare the training of a white belt vs. a black belt this becomes apparent. The more advanced you become, the fewer grips you tend to make. Quite often a beginner student's hands flail about from grip to grip, while a seasoned practitioner will make one efficient grip, and maintain it through a position. The beginner student's movements are wide and vary greatly whereas our seasoned practitioner's movements are sparse and precise. Once a student reaches around purple belt or so, they have largely learned all of the techniques they are going to know. It is their time in purple, brown and black belt to find the most efficient ways to execute these techniques, and to remove all of the excess.

It seems paradoxical to spend too many words describing the need for simplicity, and so I will avoid this at all costs. This is a simple paradigm shift, a heading for the student's compass, that should guide their actions on the mat. Less actually *is* more. When you perform the same move in fewer steps, do so. Watching guys at the highest level train, especially train as opposed to competing where there are other elements in play, it is surprising how little they actually do. They have good body position complemented by a strong grip, and they allow their training partners to do the work for them. If you put them in a compromised enough position, many guys will pass their own guards or sweep themselves. It is simply our job to give them the opportunity to do so.

In my own training, I feel my progress has been tracked by how little I have to do to meet my desired aim. Early on as a brown belt, I started to recognize that I felt as though I was doing less and less in my training, until it felt as though I was hardly doing anything at all. Good guard passing is simply getting great body position and immobilizing your partner in such a way where when they have to exaggerate their movements to advance, they pass their own guard. Good guard play is maintaining a functionally sound position with which to defend guard and off balance, and stringing together your strong position with their vulnerable lack of balance to inevitably yield a sweep.

Acquiring this skill is very similar to building a statue. Our potential lies within the uncarved block, and the only thing that lies between the block and the statue is calculated effort. The final touches in making a statue are always removing the excess, and never addition. Daily carve away the inessential from your movements, and you will find refinement that can only be added by subtraction.

As Lao Tzu taught us,

"To attain knowledge, add things every day. To attain wisdom, remove things every day."

Complementary Passions

"It is not that we have so little time but that we lose so much. ... The life we receive is not short but we make it so; we are not ill provided but use what we have wastefully."-Seneca

The fact that you are reading these words already tells me a great deal about you and brings us closer together. If you are reading this book I can safely assume many or all of the following pertain to you:

> You are a Jiu Jitsu practitioner.
>
> You are a sincere student of the art.
>
> You seek to grow and become a better version of yourself.
>
> You value education.

This, my friend, bonds us in a shared commune with an affinity toward truth that excites me greatly. We have much in common, and in these commonalities we recognize our shared brotherhood. It is in this commonality that I find the urge to implore you to seek efficiency in all your endeavors. Life, at its longest, is short. We mustn't waste any time, but time itself is too broad and impersonal a term. Truthfully, we don't have time, we have life. This subtle vocabularic change will breed far more urgency in our efforts. So, we don't have much life. Let's get going.

It would behoove the reader to, as often as possible, batch his or her interests. What I mean by this is simply to strive to have all of your endeavors complement each other. At the time of this writing, my current curriculum of study is as follows:

Jiu Jitsu

Chess

Logic Puzzles

Writing

Philosophy

Latin Root Words

The commonalities between these are clear, and this allows for accelerated growth. Consider the similarities which chess and logic puzzles share with Jiu Jitsu. These are activities which require foresight, problem solving, tactics, strategy, and efficiency in action and thought, each of which applies directly to Jiu Jitsu.

Consider my study of philosophy and Latin root words. Each of these introduce me to a better understanding of the world in which I live, and a better articulation of this understanding, both skills required in my success as a writer. At the same time, these skills lend themselves to the improvement of my ability to teach Jiu Jitsu, and as a result better learn the art myself.

Every aspect of my study improves multiple aspects of study. When I play chess, I am not just playing chess. I am getting better at Jiu Jitsu, improving my problem-solving faculties, and participating in purposeful thought. We only have so much time on this earth, and we are lucky to have the passions that we do. But our time is limited to improve upon these passions, and we must take every effort to ensure that we are consistently growing in all endeavors. This is most easily done when your passions coincide with one another. In batching your endeavors, you will find accelerated growth in each of them. With this calculated study, your potential in each will continually expand as your skills grow and exceed far beyond the medium with which you practice them.

Our time is short. Let's be sure we make the most of it.

Seek to Understand

"No man was ever wise by chance."-Seneca

In terms of our grappling, success is very often hard to quantify. There exist countless variables in every circumstance, and we rarely bring forth the attention and understanding required to make sense of what has occurred during a roll, and to learn from our experience. As a culture, we tend to err on the side of instant gratification. We assume that if we reached our desired outcome, we have succeeded. Though the outcome may not even be the end which serves us best, but even if it is, we rarely have a true understanding of the actions taken by both ourselves and our training partners to yield such an outcome.

Professor Ricardo Almeida constantly refers to the tale of Hansel and Gretel, and how we must "leave bread crumbs" so we can trace our steps and have a conscious understanding of what happens. He does this better than anybody, as his ability to recall the exact events of a training session is second to none. I believe these bread crumbs are invaluable in producing our understanding of this sport, and the bread crumbs themselves are often far more valuable than the cottage at the end of the trail.

If we go into a training session with a clear goal in mind we can be sure we will make great use of our time. "I am going to work on arm bars today," we say.

We show up at the academy, and we look for arm bars from every position. We even hit a few of them. Job well done, right? That depends. Did this focus lead to a better understanding of how the armbar works. That is the true measure of success. It is the understanding of the action that is far more valuable than the accomplishing of the action itself. Failing to perform a technique, and understanding why the failure occurred, is far more worthwhile than repeated success performed in an unconscious manner.

I always refer to the idea that the cultivation of a skill is akin to building a pyramid: the wider the base, the higher the potential peak. Our base can only be built upon the conscious understanding of *why* a technique or position is successful. It is not built off the successes themselves. I believe this is why students who become teachers make such great leaps in competency as they are forced to consciously understand what they once did on an unconscious level. Every act must be done with purpose, and we must collect data from every successful and failed attempt. The foundation of our pyramid is not built with techniques: arm bars, guard passes, and sweeps. The foundation is built upon great understanding of the underlying concepts which make these techniques possible.

A technical accomplishment on the mat is only an accomplishment when it leads to further successes. For this to be the case, we must seek to understand our endeavor above all else. Leave yourself a trail of bread crumbs, and connect the dots on your way to technical mastery. An arm bar in a vacuum is worthless. It is the realization of the truths which constitute that arm bar that is the real treasure we seek.

Do not seek victory, for victory in itself will not serve you. Seek to understand what made the victory possible. Then the world is yours!

Win the Battle or Win the War

"No thing great is created suddenly, any more than a bunch of grapes or a fig. If you tell me that you desire a fig, I answer you that there must be time. Let it first blossom, then bear fruit, then ripen."-Epictetus

In Jiu Jitsu, such as in life, we often find ourselves at the crossroads of finding success in the immediate, or delaying victory today under the umbrella of achieving a larger goal in the future. Whether or not we are aware of it, we are making this choice. And if we are not aware of it, we are choosing to win the battle today and neglecting the war of our lives. This is a decision that all great men and women consciously make, and we must follow suit.

We tend to get tunnel vision in the present moment where nothing else exists but the task at hand. Truthfully, this is one of the greatest benefits of martial arts, or any activity for that matter. If we are confined to the present moment with laser-like focus, we are free of the anxieties of tomorrow and the baggage of the past. Freedom from the thinking mind is our underlying goal for most of human activity, and this is good. Until, it is not.

Sometimes we get so lost in the present that we forget our desired end. This is why we must have a predetermined goal for each and every training session. It is far too easy to simply show up, train hard, and feel like you improved. We have to be smarter than this. If you simply put your head down and put forth effort, you will certainly get better. But to what degree, and in what area? We each have a certain set of skills, and when met with adversity we will rely on these skills to succeed. In a competition, we want the best desired outcome in that moment, so relying on our strengths is the appropriate response. This may not always be the case in training.

If my weakness is passing the guard to my right, and I have a clear focus of the purpose of the training session, I will pass right. I will meet with adversity, but when I do I will remember why I am there and I will persevere. It will be difficult and there is a high probability of failure, but this is purposeful failure. It is a conscious choice. I am actively choosing in what area of my training I wish to grow, and I will grow accordingly. This is having the end in mind.

Conversely, if I just show up and train hard, the paradigm completely shifts. My main focus is to succeed in the present moment, and in doing so I will use whatever techniques will lead to this fulfillment. Being driven by the moment, I will play to my strengths and almost assuredly pass left. Now, I am still training hard and I did in fact pass the guard. In a vacuum, this is an accomplishment. But is that the accomplishment I really need? If I am a competent guard passer, and I always pass left, and I know I can pass left, am I really improving by passing left? Probably not, and if I am it is minimal.

This one microcosm is an expression of the whole. We have to have an idea of where we want to improve before we put ourselves in these positions. Autopilot is great, and removal of thought is one of the highest ideals of training. But removal of thought in the moment must be preceded by purposeful thought beforehand.

In the previous chapter we said that the acquisition of a skill is similar to the building of a pyramid. The wider the base, the higher the potential peak. Too often we spend time in the upper levels of the pyramid, honing techniques of which we already have a good understanding. We do this because it is fun to succeed, and because it comes naturally. It is easy. But to achieve the greatest final product, we must build out, not up. We do so by consciously addressing our weaknesses outside of training, and purposefully fine tuning them in training.

Continuing with the building analogies, consider one final point:

Every day is a brick. Now, a brick by itself has little utility, but bricks put together in a complementary way can change the world. When we pursue victory in the battle as opposed to the war, we are awarded a brick in its solitary state. There is nothing to combine it with, and so it serves little purpose. We do this daily, monthly, and yearly, and we find a slew of bricks across the ground with few if any strengthening connections.

But when we begin in each day with the end in mind, the bricks are woven together and stacked upon one another. These bricks quickly become a wall, and the daily choices of pursuing a higher ideal lead to a monument worthy of our efforts. This is the difference we must have in our lives.

Have a clear-cut plan on what you wish to improve, and seek opportunities to improve it. The more conscious and honest we can be about our shortcomings, the more strength we will have to improve them. We are going to train hard anyway, we are not going to sweat any more or less. It is simply imperative that the sweat is properly directed.

Learning

"Experience teaches only the teachable..."-Aldous Huxley

The most valuable skill one can learn is learning *how* to learn. This is the skill which precedes the acquisition of all other skills, and must be the bedrock upon which one builds their life. When you learn *how* to learn, all human activities become possible. The beautiful truth about learning is that it remains unchanged regardless of the vehicle with which it is being exercised. The acquisition of any knowledge comes by a very simple feedback loop. In our sciences classes at school, we learned about the scientific method. It was boring, seemed pointless, and most of us cannot remember any of its constituents after Hypothesis.

We must remember that science is a way of using empirical evidence to better understand our world. We are all scientists, just many of us are not very good ones. However, we are all capable of exercising our intellects in a purposeful, linear pursuit of knowledge. Let's take a trip down memory lane and for the first time since high school entertain the notions of the scientific method:

> *Observation* -We see something which
>
> intrigues us.

Question -We ask a question. Why does this occur? What is it? What are the contributing factors?

Research -We study to better understand the phenomenon.

Hypothesis -We make a prediction.

Experiment -We test the prediction.

Collect Data -We record the results of our experiment.

Analysis -We interpret our data.

Conclusion -We compare/contrast our hypothesis with our findings. Distillation of results. Identify trends or associations.

This is a very simplified description of the scientific method, but serves our purposes here. Essentially, we have a theory that we use to make a prediction, we design an experiment to test that prediction, we perform the experiment and with our new-found knowledge we determine if what we have found is supportive of our thoughts.

It may not seem like it, but this is the exact process you use every time you are training Jiu Jitsu. We are all scientists, and the better we are able to utilize the scientific method in our training, the greater our acquisition of skill. In keeping this Jiu Jitsu specific, many of us are very competent in all but the final two steps. On the whole, we are very good at practicing the scientific method until we reach the moment of *Analysis*. Remember, great science is largely advanced in the accurate interpretation of data. Great data without proper analysis is worthless. We must derive meaning from our findings. Every time we train we run experiments, but we rarely learn from these experiments!

Let's consider the scientific method again in reference to Jiu Jitsu:

> *Observation* - My butterfly guard is horrendous.
>
> *Question* - What is the best way to play butterfly guard?
>
> *Research* - We watch film on Marcelo Garcia.
>
> *Hypothesis* - We believe we now know how to play butterfly guard. (A hypothesis is a testable prediction. Think "If/Then." If I do 'x', then my butterfly guard will be more effective.)
>
> *Experiment* - We try it in training.
>
> *Collect Data* - Every moment we play butterfly guard we are collecting data.
>
> ***Analysis*** -
>
> *Conclusion* - We now decide whether a particular implementation of playing butterfly guard is more effective than what we did

before.

Following this linear progression, we see just how important and vast the Analysis stage becomes. This is everything! Without analysis, we can never come to a clear understanding of our findings. This is the area that seems to trip up most Jiu Jitsu practitioners. We can often seem to understand what happens in a roll, but too often we mistake the understanding of what for the understanding of why it happened. The whats are easy. "This sweep worked." "This sweep did not." The whys are considerably more complicated, and as a result the understanding of what to why follows parallel with the skill of white belt to black belt.

It is not enough to say, "That butterfly sweep works!" and conclude that you have now added a successful tool to your arsenal. You must address *why* it worked:

I had a strong overhook.

I took away my partner's post.

I was on my one hip and not neutral.

I had good head position below my partner's.

I fell to the side and not straight back.

I pushed off the ground with my bottom leg.

I got my ear to the mat.

I kept a strong butterfly hook through the entire move.

My partner's weight was coming into me at the

time of the sweep.

My partner's weight was coming into me because I originally pushed into him first.

This is "why" the sweep works, and it is this proper analysis that leads to accurate and beneficial conclusions. With proper analysis like this, we are afforded the opportunity to compound our knowledge by bringing it into future experiments. We are able to connect the dots and find corollaries between various techniques that lead to success. This is one of the major turning points in any practitioner's journey toward mastery. The degree with which we can analyze our findings is directly proportional to the progress we will experience. I say again. We are all scientists. We all seek to better understand Jiu Jitsu through the use of this method. If we are going to do it anyway, we might as well make an effort to better consciously understand the mechanisms with which we do so. The experiments are the fun part. We all love to train. But what we do with our findings, that is what separates the wheat from the chaff, and ensures we are making the most of our time.

Once we embrace the scientific method, we find a clear and concise roadmap with which to learn this beautiful art.

Thought Exercise

The Parable of Fish and Water

From David Foster Wallace's 2005 Commencement Address at Kenyon College

"...There are these two young fish swimming along and they happen to meet an older fish swimming the other way, who nods at them and says 'Morning, boys. How's the water?' And the two young fish swim on for a bit, and then eventually one of them looks over at the other and goes 'What the hell is water?'"

What does the water represent, and do we recognize it in our daily lives?

Part III - Swinging the Ax

"A sword by itself does not slay; it is merely the weapon used by the slayer."-Seneca

Limit Variables

"Our life is frittered away by detail. An honest man has hardly need to count more than his ten fingers, or in extreme cases he may add his ten toes, and lump the rest. Simplicity, simplicity, simplicity! I say, let your affairs be as two or three, and not a hundred or a thousand; instead of a million count half a dozen, and keep your accounts on your thumb nail."-Henry David Thoreau

Many of us have heard the idea of paralysis by choice. The more options we have, the harder it becomes to choose one. Consider the last time you went food shopping. You walk down the pasta aisle to simply pick up some pasta for dinner. You know you want pasta, and you have found the pasta aisle. This should be easy, right? Not so fast. In front of you lie shelves that run the entire length of the aisle, from feet to hairline, filled with a wide assortment of pasta. Fusilli. Angel Hair. Rotini. Whole wheat. Gluten free. Veggie-based. Store brand. Organic. The choices go on forever. A minute ago you were certain what you desired, and now you are lost. With today's advancing abundance and specifications, we encounter this problem whenever we look to make any change in our lives. Jiu Jitsu is no different.

There are countless variables to any sequence of techniques in a Jiu Jitsu position.

I do this, and then my partner will do this. But then if I do this, he may do this. But when I do this instead, he responds like this. Etcetera, etcetera.

Often in Jiu Jitsu, if you think, you have already lost. We are not afforded the time to, mid-roll, assess the situation and determine the possible variables. We must have a predetermined plan. We must know our action, and know the most likely corresponding reactions from our opponent, and then know our action to their reaction. Notice I say action. We are acting, they are re-acting, and there is a vast difference.

It is this logical, linear attempt at understanding the sequence of events that yields to our most desired result. As the old saying goes, "Make things as simple as you can, but not simpler."

Whatever technique we want to use, it behooves us to understand the potential circumstances that will occur post its use. If I do 'A,' my partner will most likely do 1, 2, or 3. If my partner does 1, I will do 'a.' If my partner does 2, I will do 'b,' etc, etc. If we can automate our actions, we remove the thinking mind from the equation and vastly speed up our computing power and consequent actions. There are an infinite amount of variables in Jiu Jitsu. You can train every moment of every day of your life, and never have the same roll twice. We cannot prepare for all possible outcomes, but we can prepare for the most common.

Consider the following example.

We are mounted, and are looking to recover guard. We know that when we upa, most of the time one of two things will happen. Either our partner will post their lead leg, or their back leg. Knowing this going in, we already have a predetermined course of action for how we will act after our partner's response. If he posts the lead leg, we will knee-elbow escape back to guard. If he posts the back leg, we will hip escape toward it and recover over-under guard. Our actions become automatic, and we do not waste precious moments in thought.

In Jiu Jitsu an inch is a mile, and a second is an eternity. Use each wisely.

The greater an understanding of each of our chosen attacks, and the corresponding most common responses (generally no more than two or three) we may encounter, the more we can make our efforts in Jiu Jitsu a predetermined success rather than chance. And we do not have to understand this for all possible positions. This would be ideal, but is unrealistic (especially for the Jiu Jitsu hobbiest). We are creatures of habit, and tend to spend much of our time training in only a handful of positions, using only a handful of techniques. If we simply understand the most occurring situations in our training, our efforts will yield much in the ways of our growth as Jiu Jitsu practitioners.

Consider your favorite few positions. Consider the

reactions you most commonly find and address them beforehand.

As the old sayings go, failing to prepare is preparing to fail, but luck is when preparation meets opportunity.

Newtonian Jiu Jitsu

"For every action there is an equal and opposite re-action."- Isaac Newton's Third Law of Motion

This coincides perfectly with the previous chapter, *Limit Variables*.

Every action has an equal and opposite reaction. This is such an obvious understanding of the world that only our brightest could have first realized it. Isaac Newton changed the way in which we view the modern world and has no rival in his interpretation of natural philosophy. Little did he know as he meandered about the United Kingdom in the 17th century, that he also gave us one of the most important concepts in efficient Jiu Jitsu. Long-limbed coupled with unrivaled intelligence, Isaac himself may have become great in Jiu Jitsu had he been given the opportunity; at the very least we can safely assume he would have had a nasty Dela Riva guard.

Every action has an equal and opposite reaction. This in my mind is the quintessential motto for grappling. Very simply, in whatever direction we wish to move our opponent, you can be sure they will resist with equivalent opposition. If I try to push my partner away, he will pull himself closer. If I try to pull my opponent closer, he will assuredly push away. This is a simple idea, but if you understand it it will serve you well.

If I am playing guard on bottom, the very best thing my opponent on top can do is give me their weight. Once I have that, I will be able to manipulate their position into an advantaged position of my own. But people are smart. If I want my opponent's weight, and I pull my partner, he will resist. I have shown my hand, and will not likely get a chance to redeem myself in that moment without great effort. Think of this in the context of relationships. When courting another, quite often their least attractive quality is when they reciprocate our affection. As the old saying goes, "I would never want to be in a club that would have me as a member." We must be smarter than this.

All of Jiu Jitsu is finding a way to get your partner to willingly go where you want him to go in the first place.

Rather than pull my partner, I will push him away. I will actively attempt to send him in the opposite direction of where I want him, knowing that he will counter my motives. As I push him away, he will drive back equally and resist my attempt. As he drives back in, he is willingly advancing toward my desired position for him. He is doing the work for me. Consider again relationships. As childish as it is, we often pretend not to be interested in the party which we are, so that they become interested in us. It is our aversion that leads to their affection. Jiu Jitsu is no different.

Wherever I want my opponent to go, I will not try to

bring them there. It is effort-laden, they are skillful and smart. This is inefficient. Rather, send your partner in the opposite direction, fight their movement toward where you want them, and they will strive with great force to arrive at the destination you had wished for them in the first place.

Isaac Newton had grappling figured out long ago, and it is time we heed his words!

Opposing Attacks

"Really, the fundamental, ultimate mystery -- the only thing you need to know to understand the deepest metaphysical secrets -- is this: that for every outside there is an inside and for every inside there is an outside, and although they are different, they go together."-Alan Watts

So now we have a clear understanding of the need to limit variables in our training and the concept of equal and opposite reaction. Now we turn to the uber-specific need of having opposing threats, and nowhere is that better described than in Homer's *Odyssey*. While traversing the strait, Odysseus must make a choice between two evils. He must pass by Scylla, a six-headed sea monster with each head capable of devouring one of his men, or Charybdis, a giant whirlpool capable of destroying the entire ship. Either way, Odysseus and his men must suffer at the hands of fate. It is believed that this was the original version of the expression, "Between a rock and a hard place."

Much as sailors were forced to choose between two evils, so shall your contemporaries feel, should you adopt this mode of practice, when training with you. If you can create these situations in multiple positions, you are already at the upper echelon of Jiu Jitsu practitioners.

Consider your greatest attacks. What are your go-to

submissions? Sweeps? Guard passes? We all have certain areas of a high level of competency, so this shouldn't be hard. But now the real question, do you know that technique's opposite? More clearly stated, do you know what technique opposes your current technique with dichotomic splendor?

None of our attacks should exist by themselves on an island. If this is the case and it fails, you have accomplished nothing and are in a constant state of reset. All of our attacks must chain together if we wish to practice Jiu Jitsu in a truly artful sense. Keeping with our Odyssey analogy, many of us have a Scylla. We all have go to moves that we feel we can get most of the time. But, do we have a complementary Charybdis? Do you have a technique which your partner directly moves toward while moving away from the other? Like a ping pong ball being volleyed back and forth, so shall your opponent feel when you have opposing attacks.

Imagine a continuum in which on the far left side is a technique which requires your partner's weight coming into you. Now, on the opposite end of the continuum lies an opposing technique from the same position, in which it is required for your opponent's weight to be moving away from you. By having these polar ends, no matter what direction your partner chooses, he is working toward an outcome which best serves you.

If he defends the "weight coming in" technique, by sheer lack of options he must be advancing toward your "weight going away" technique. And when he avoids the "weight going away" technique by driving back in, he is setting himself up for your "weight coming in" technique. This holds true over all areas of Jiu Jitsu, and the best practitioners recognize this. Watch a truly technical practitioner train. It looks like a constant ebb and flow between two distant points, and only when the aim can be effortlessly achieved (only when his partner has gone all the way toward one end of the continuum) does he strike.

This way of practice is efficient and beautiful. This is the art in martial arts.

When you have achieved this mindset in training, much of the difficulties of grappling have been removed.

Minimum Viable Product

"It is vain to do with more what can be done with less."-William of Occam

In product development, a common phrase tossed around by entrepreneurs is "Minimum Viable Product." Wikipedia, as of 4/1/2015 defines the MVP as such:

"The minimum viable product is that version of a new product which allows a team to collect the maximum amount of validated learning about customers with the least effort."

This is a unique paradigm shift. Far too often, businesses and individuals fail to produce because they are too busy trying to be perfect. They keep their product (or themselves) on hold in a pursuit of perfection rather than going out into the world and collecting invaluable experience and data. The "MVP" tells us to do the opposite. This philosophy teaches us to leave safe harbor for the rough seas of real-world experience, and to accept that a rough copy out in the world serves us far greater than a masterpiece sitting quietly on our shelves.

Eric Reis, founder of IMVU Inc. and considered by many the pioneer of the lean start-up movement, wrote extensively about the concept of the Minimum Viable Product in his book, *The Lean Start Up.*

Upon reading this book, my first thought was not, "How can I create my own product to make millions of dollars?" It was far simpler. I asked myself, "How can I relate this concept to Jiu Jitsu?" It was this question that changed the way I would forever look at this art.

In keeping with the modus operandi of the MVP, I considered the positions and techniques of Jiu Jitsu. What was the absolute least I had to do to get toward where I want to go. Channeling Vilfredo Pareto's "80/20" rule (80% of results tend to come from 20% of the effort), I sought the most efficient means of accomplishing my desired intent with the least action possible. My learning, and technical ability, accelerated greatly as I found these ever-apparent fundamentals in every position.

Again, what is the one golden rule to hold onto in each position? What is the most important part of the technique? What is the 20% of the actions that leads to 80% of the results?

Someone keeps turtling as you are passing their guard. Control the bottom elbow. Someone keeps recovering guard from side control. Do not let their knee and elbow connect. You keep getting submitted inside the guard. Keep your posture. You are having trouble passing the guard. Just get chest to chest.

These "MVPs" exist everywhere, and I think it is essential to our progress as students to become aware of them, and keep them in our conscious attention until it is no longer necessary. In many positions in Jiu Jitsu there seems to be a great "rule of thumb" that if you hold onto, you will avoid many of the vicissitudes of the common grappler. This is not being lazy, or looking for an easy way out. This is calculated precision and efficiency.

The economist E.F. Schumacher said, "Any intelligent fool can make things bigger, more complex, and more violent. It takes a touch of genius—and a lot of courage to move in the opposite direction." Mastery is a movement toward the simple. The greater degree to which we can break things down to the essentials while removing our focus from the trivial, the more beneficial our practice would be. It appears, at least from my perspective, that each and every position in Jiu Jitsu regardless of the seeming complexity is really governed by no more than a handful of minimum viable products. Pursue to understand these essentials, and you will see that complexity is a myth perpetuated by lack of understanding, and it is this understanding which is possible for each of us. We just need to know where to look!

Be the Sphere

"Don't get set into one form, adapt it and build your own, and let it grow, be like water. Empty your mind, be formless, shapeless-- like water. Now you put water in a cup, it becomes the cup; You put water into a bottle it becomes the bottle; You put it in a teapot it becomes the teapot. Now water can flow or it can crash. Be water, my friend."-Bruce Lee

If there is one distinction between advanced and beginner students that stands out above any other, it is the effortless body control and smoothness through movements of the advanced student. Mastery is a movement toward simplicity, and it is a movement of rounding out the edges, of turning the cube into a sphere.

Consider a white belt:

They are tense, and rigid. There is no connection between their movements as each advancement occurs in isolation. I liken their actions to rolling a cube. The cube has clear distinctions between each side, hard 90 degree angles, and rigid boundaries. When we roll it from side to side, it is final and definite. You start rolling it, and it tilts on its side and then falls violently to a new side on which it pauses. Then again. It begins to turn, you tilt it on its hard edge, and it crashes back down with a clash. There is no sequence in movement. It is choppy. Ugly.

Consider a black belt:

They are loose, and flowing. They have complete sequencing between movements as one flows after the other. So much so that the illusion of separate movements dissipates, and their actions coalesce into a continuous dance. They roll as if they are a sphere. Effortless, continuous motion with no clear boundary between positions. You cannot tell where one "side" ends and the other begins, because there are no segments in the chain. Their movement has merged into one homogeneous exercise.

This is the most glaring difference between practitioners along the training continuum. In all areas, we must seek to chisel off the corners as we learn to roll rather than stumble around. It is the removal of this rigidness that allows for one's Jiu Jitsu to flow together like waves. Embody the idea of the sphere. In all of your drilling and sparring, avoid moving erratically and choppy. Seek to roll and transition from position to position without any clear distinction between the two.

Chisel off all the excess and become the sphere.

After all, why do you think we call it "rolling?"

Wu Wei

"The Way is ever without action, Yet nothing is left undone."- Lao Tzu, Tao Te Ching

Of all the Eastern philosophies, I have particular affinity for Taoism. Commonly misunderstood and widely shrugged off as spiritual jargon, this has been one of the most impactful ideologies I have ever come across. The *Tao Te Ching* (pronounced Dow-Day-Ching), written by Lao Tzu around the time of the Buddha and the Ancient Greeks, consists of 81 short chapters teaching on various aspects of experience such as emptiness, knowledge, presence, and the concept of Wu Wei.

Wu Wei is translated as "non-doing" or "without effort." In Taoism, it is the application of Wu Wei that brings one in accordance with the Tao (translated as "the way"). This concept of without effort is expressed in Jiu Jitsu at its highest levels. If you watch a truly great practitioner play, it appears as though he is doing nothing, and yet everything is accomplished. There is no sense of great physical strain or effort on their part, and somehow they effortlessly manipulate their partner to their desire. This lack of effort is the single most apparent distinction between the beginning and advanced student.

Much of Western thought has given us the idea that if we just try hard enough we can accomplish anything.

This paradigm is reflected in the way in which we treat our own selves, each other, and the world of which we are a part. I talked at length about effort in the original *My Mastery*, and it remains to be one of the virtues I most admire in others. Nothing great in the material world is ever achieved without effort, but there is an equal need for a lack of effort, especially in the immaterial world. Spiritual teachers often talk about effort as actually the obstacle to the attainment of higher metaphysical ideals. The same holds true for Jiu Jitsu.

We acknowledge that the highest expression of technique is that of "Wu Wei," effortless action. It is the power and beauty of this mode of practice that attracts so many of us, and has us all pursuing mastery to whatever extent our circumstances allow. Speaking in generalities, we can measure the value of a particular technique in a particular setting based off the effort that is required to achieve its end. As we gain greater experience, we recognize when we execute a technique in just the right way at just the right time, it truly is effortless. One of my favorite aspects of teaching is to see a white belt experience this for the first time, and to watch the sheer amazement and joy on their faces. They have for the first time just experienced what Jiu Jitsu can be, and once they feel this they become hooked.

I am reminded of the Zen Koan depicting this concept in a conversation between a young monk and his master:

"Master, said the young monk, How long will it take me to reach Enlightenment?"

"Hmmm, about 10 years," replied the master.

The young monk was determined as he responded, "But sir, I am unlike all the other monks. I will work twice as hard as anyone else."

"OK then," replied the master, "Make that 20 years."

Frustrated and bewildered, the young monk states, "Then I will work harder. Day and night I will devote myself entirely toward this aim."

Finally the wise master replies, "Then you will never reach it."

In Jiu Jitsu, we often fall into the trap of simply trying a technique "harder," rather than recognizing that it is a poorly chosen tool for the task at hand. Often trying harder is simply just pushing us farther in the wrong direction, much like the student from the above story. In the beginning, the white belt is often simply attempting a technique, but in the wrong way. Hence, they pursue the fruitless path of simply trying harder. For the advanced student, it is often not that they are performing the technique poorly, but that they are attempting it at the wrong time, in the wrong setting. The resulting effort with which they try to make up for this shortcoming often leads them farther down the wrong rabbit hole.

Effort is a great virtue and will serve us well in life. Equally so will a lack of effort. Much of the higher life, whether it be the practice of a martial art or chosen skill, or navigating the immaterial world of the mind in search of peace and calm, is guided by its opposite, a lack of effort. The Eastern philosophies teach a great deal about detachment, the act of letting go.

In Buddhism, it is when we detach ourselves from desires that we find a cessation of suffering. Effort and detachment cannot coincide. One cannot "try real hard" to let go in the immaterial world just as in the material. Imagine you pick up a heavy dumbbell, and I say to you, "Alright dear friend, Let go." You drop the weight and it comes crashing to the ground. Now I ask you to pick it up again, and this time I say, "Job well done, my good man. Now, this time I want to see you *really* try to drop that weight." You drop it, and nothing really changes. Now I ask for a final time, "OK now, as if your life depended on it, and the lives of everyone you know and love, Drop the weight!!!" You drop it, and feel no real difference from the first time. This is a physical example of an action where no amount of effort can complete the task as it is only a lack of effort, a letting go, that will achieve its aim.

In Eastern philosophies and modern spirituality, we are taught to let go of the ego. We see that as we cling, so are we bound. One cannot try to let go of the ego, because it is the very ego which does the trying. That is an act moving us farther down the rabbit hole. It is the removal of effort, the letting go, that frees us of the ego.

In Jiu Jitsu, we tend to have operational biases with which we navigate each role. We favor a particular set of techniques, and we do our best to guide the roll into positions where we can effectively execute those techniques. We do not hold complete competency over every technique in every situation, and so we limit the variables to those which we are best suited to address. As a result, we tend to force techniques in the improper setting, and in doing so put forth great effort. Imagine a true master of the art, someone with complete skill in every aspect of Jiu Jitsu. This master would not force anything. He would simply allow the roll to take whatever form it does, and in every position would act in the most efficient way based off what the circumstance dictates, and not what he himself prefers.

Due to our lack of universal competency, we are not afforded this luxury. We put forth effort and try harder at inopportune times because often this is the only choice we have. This is a fine mode of practice for now, but we mustn't stay here too long. We must maintain the goal of practicing this art in its highest form, Wu Wei. Mastery is a movement from complexity to simplicity, as well as a movement from effort to the effortless.

We must not learn to try harder. The key is to learn

how not to try in the first place.

Pursue Your Training Partner's Skills

"The cave you fear to enter holds the treasure that you seek."- Joseph Campbell

As talked about in the chapter *Win the Battle or Win the War*, we far too often strive to succeed in the moment while neglecting our greatest good. This is perfectly logical as we pursue the path of least resistance on our way to our desired success within the training session, but this will not yield our greatest gains. In order to be as efficient as possible with our training, we must put ourselves in the most difficult positions during training. The harder the conflict, the greater the gains it will yield.

This is where we must spend as much time as possible in the comfort zones of our training partners. In order to get the most possible growth, we must find the area in which our training partner has the greatest degree of skill relative to our own. This turning point came one day when I was training with my good friend, Garry Tonon. If you are reading this, you probably know who he is. On the outside chance that you do not, he is a 2x world champion and has won nearly every tournament there is. Widely considered the best American light weight grappler, Garry's grappling ability is only rivaled by his kindness, and absolutely one-of-a-kind way in which he views the world. He is a madman, and I mean that in the best sense of the word. I digress.

Garry has some of the best leg locks in the world, and so it made perfect sense that when I would train with Garry my goal would be to not get leg locked. But I was missing the point! He is such an incredible resource, and I was not making the most of this opportunity. Why run from his greatest skill (especially in training) when this skill could lead to my own? Instead, the switch flipped in my head and I decided I would *only* pursue leg locks when training with Garry. Obviously, this approach does not fare well for me, but I am collecting invaluable data that I was otherwise avoiding. This is where the lesson took shape.

Wherever your training partners are great, no matter how far their skill surpasses yours in that area, *especially* when their skill surpasses yours in that area, that is where you should try to spend most of your time training with them. This yields the greatest results. If your teammate has a great Dela Riva guard, try to only pass standing in their Dela Riva guard! If they have great scrambles, try to out-scramble the scrambler. This is the surefire way to get the most out of your training, and lead to tremendous growth.

We are very fortunate to have the resources that we do in our training partners. It is about time we be as resourceful as we can with those resources. Wherever your training partners strengths, meet them there and that strength will soon become yours!

Learn a Game to Learn Its Defense

"I destroy my enemies when I make them my friends."-
Abraham Lincoln

Sound advice in life. Equally sound in Jiu Jitsu.

The duality of Jiu Jitsu is a beautiful thing, as you can never learn any aspect of it in isolation. If you are learning how to attack, you are tacitly learning its defense, and if you are learning to defend, you are implicitly learning to attack. Our studies always compound upon themselves to yield more growth than that which we consciously seek. This has brought me to one of the simplest concepts that I have devoted a great deal of training toward:

If you want to learn how to defend something, you must learn how to attack with that very technique.

Perfect example:

I am commonly asked by students of all ranks, "How do I defend leg locks?" My best advice has been, and will continue to be, start going for them yourself. It is only when we learn the intricacies of how the attacks work, that we truthfully learn the intricacies of the defense. Around my time as an early Brown Belt, I was made very much aware of my ignorance in the leg lock game. I had been caught in a tournament with an inverted heel hook, and I decided to derive the lesson of learning from my mistakes. I sought out my teammates to better understand the leg lock game, and found that my best progress toward knowledge was made in the way of understanding them myself.

Luckily I had access to the likes of Ricardo Almeida, Tom Deblass, Garry Tonon and Gordon Ryan. I quickly fell in love with the fine subtleties of the game, and how just like as in all areas of Jiu Jitsu, the difference was made in millimeters. I dove in headfirst in an attempt to add leg locks to my own attacks, and in doing so I was learning the way in which to defend them.

This holds true for all areas of Jiu Jitsu. If you are getting beat with something, whatever it is, start implementing that technique in your own game, and soon all will become clear. If you are getting triangled on a regular basis, start going for triangles yourself. If you are getting under-the-leg guard passed, then spend a month or so only looking for that in your own passing game. You will be amazed at your progress as you not only learn the defense to your previous weakness, but you cultivate a game in which you are highly skilled in an area which was once so foreign.

For most of us, the move we are getting killed with today will be our "go-to" six months from now. When you learn all the details regarding attacking with a technique, you will learn its defense simultaneously. Pursue understanding of your weakness, and it will soon fail to be such!

The Importance of Guard-Oriented Training

"The art of being wise is the art of knowing what to overlook." -William James

I tend to write in a more abstract and conceptual way, but the following is an idea I deemed worthy of specific attention. There are a variety of positions in Jiu Jitsu, but they are largely boiled down into the major four: guard, side control, mount, and back. There are varying degrees and types of each position, but for simplicity sake the positions of this art can be summarized in this way. To be uber specific, we recognize that for each of these positions there exists both poles. We have playing the guard or passing the guard, attacking from side control, mount or back, as well as the defending of these positions. In essence, there are essentially eight major aspects of the positional hierarchy.

Upon first glance, it may seem pragmatic to spend an equal time mastering each position to ensure all our bases are covered. In theory this makes sense, as we want to be well rounded with no glaring skill discrepancies in our game. Though in a vacuum this appears sound, we must look deeper into this idea. When training with someone of equivalent skill, nearly the entirety of the roll takes place within the guard, whether top or bottom.

Since among our peers this is the position which occupies the vast majority of our training, it is this position that is deserving of the most attention. I believe that nearly all of our training should be focused on playing guard and passing guard. Yes, we must be skilled in all aspects of training, but equally so we must make the most of our limited time training.

If we spend our time developing great skill playing guard, then our need for solid defense in side control, mount, or the back becomes increasingly unnecessary. Any advanced student will tell you the best way to recover guard is simply not to get your guard passed in the first place.

In regard to top position, yes the ability to attack from these advantageous positions is paramount, but it does not matter how great our attacks from side control or mount are if we cannot get there in the first place. I believe, in the context of this art, that having a great guard and great guard passing should be the main concern for the majority of practitioners. If you have a great guard, and solid leg lock defense, you become virtually invincible on bottom. Conversely, if you have great guard passing on top, you will not have to worry about the only two dangers of being swept or submitted. Realistically, the only ways we end up defending side control or mount is when we allow our guard to be passed, or we are swept into these positions. Acquiring great skill in passing and playing guard negates these aspects of training.

At the higher levels with similarly skilled training partners or opponents, much of our time is spent in the guard. Whether top or bottom, it behooves the serious practitioner to devote much of their practice to this one facet of training. Once again we consider the "80/20" rule in the pursuit of proper time allocation, and it becomes clear that the biggest bang for our buck is focusing on the guard.

A final thought:

The positional hierarchy is meant as a blueprint to follow with the inevitable finality of a submission. Many would say that the sequence of sweep, pass, submit is the essence of Jiu Jitsu. The submission is a major aspect of Jiu Jitsu, and one which is deserving of much attention. But I stress again the importance of considering these concepts when practicing with someone of equivalent skill. Very rarely do we see a submission off one's back when training with a true peer, and even rarer still do we see this in the high levels of competition ranging from IBJJF to the UFC. The majority of submissions come from top position, and are only made possible once we have moved past the guard. Positional advancement, in my mind, should be the sole focus of the beginning to intermediate practitioner. While avoiding at all costs limiting ourselves, I think there are truly very few practitioners who will ever really be great at submitting off their back when training within someone of equal skill. The gi does make these submissions more accessible, but I think most of the readers will certainly see this truth in no gi.

This being the case, at least through my lens, proves the necessity of focusing on playing and passing the guard.

Competition

"Competition has been shown to be useful up to a certain point and no further, but cooperation, which is the thing we must strive for today, begins where competition leaves off." - Franklin D. Roosevelt

The following is my interpretation of Jiu Jitsu competition. I feel this topic consumes the mind of many Jiu Jitsu practitioners, and its significance is not matched with an equivalent devotion of discussion. It is time competition is paid the attention that it is already given, but in an analytical way.

I believe *everyone* should compete in something at one point in their lives. I have competed in athletics for twenty years, and it has been one of the most beneficial experiences of my life. I derived a sense of self early on in my life from sports, and it was the challenges I faced on the field that prepared me for the challenges in life. When I think back on all of the athletic experiences I have had, I can see clearly how much they shaped who I have become.

In baseball, pitching in Little League all-star games, which as far as I was concerned was Game 7 of the World Series, taught me at a young age to perform on a grand stage. Playing high school football on Saturday mornings, with the whole school watching every play, taught me accountability and pride while giving me an identity through the whirlwind of high school emotions. Competing in MMA fights and Jiu Jitsu tournaments has given me the ability to devote my life to a cause, and put my head down and work until a task is achieved. It's taught me to rise up in moments of adversity, and has taught me how to deal with both victory and defeat.

Competition allows us to look within ourselves in times of great struggle, and shows us what we are made of. Quite often the opportunity brings something outside of us that we never knew existed. It gives us the chance to perform under great pressure while at great risk. Competition affords us the growth that its maniacal dedication requires. While competing in my early 20s, martial arts gave me a heading for my compass, a definitive purpose which steered me clear of the ever-so-common distractions that 20-something Americans face. It taught me above all, that I had the ability to doggedly work toward a goal and achieve it.

Competition as a vehicle for self-discovery and personal growth is an invaluable tool for anyone, regardless of what they are competing in. But it is not without pitfalls. The growth it yields is purely contingent upon your relationship with competing itself. If you derive a sense of self from beating others, from always being the best, you will never be enough. There will always be somebody who beats you, and there will always be another tournament to win. There is an odd paradox that no one talks about regarding the victory-driven mindset of competition.

We set a goal, say, to win a tournament. We strive with might and main, day after day, as we focus with tunnel vision on our goal. We are constantly referring to a future event, and we neglect the present moment. Everything is working toward that aim. Everything is looking toward the future. Then the tournament arrives, and we are competing with complete focus in the present moment. So much focus in fact, that our selves disappear in the pursuit of victory as we switch on to autopilot. Even while competing, we are still working toward that victory, still looking toward the future. If we are fortunate, we win. But then all of a sudden, that thing we were working toward and focusing on for the past few months, is over. It's in the past, and now we (even minutes after our final match) are looking back at our accomplishment. It's not something we are doing now, it's something we have done. And so we spend months of our lives neglecting the present moment while looking forward, and then in an instant, it is all behind us and we have no real relationship with the present moment. Technically, we never get to experience that win (when I say we, I mean the self you most commonly identify with, the "I"), and it is often followed by a letdown, a "Now what?" feeling.

For the very few who are fortunate enough to make a living from competition, they are in the minority and for obvious reasons have a very different relationship with competition than your common amateur. For the rest of us, I personally believe someone should compete as long as they enjoy it and are growing from the experience. If it is a vehicle toward becoming a better version of yourself, it is often worth the sacrifice.

I think it's important to remember that the healthiest relationship is not to compete against another, but to compete against one's self. Its not about beating others, it's about being better than who you were when you woke up that morning. We get confused by the language, and due to the word "competition" we often develop an us vs. them mentality. This is the type of outlook that leads to a flood of vice and aggression. At a certain point, at least for most of us, we learn that we no longer have to compete against others. We recognize that beating another will not bring us peace, and we more so use competition as a means of personal growth. This is the worthwhile use of competition post the adolescent age.

At a certain point in an athlete's life, we all stop competing. We all do this for a variety of reasons, but we will all do this eventually. The great philosopher Alan Watts famously said, "When you get the message, hang up the phone." This motto applies to all areas of life, certainly grappling competition. I believe many of us are drawn to competition for reasons of self-worth, seeing what we are made of, showing the world who be perceive ourselves to be, or simply as a challenge. I think once we have tasted these aims, once we have "gotten the message," it is probably wise to hang up the phone. Maybe we pick it back up from time to time to remind ourselves of the lessons we have learned, or to make sure we are still the person we wish to be, but its probably not best to sit around on hold forever.

For me personally, I haven't competed in over a year, and that's not to say I will not again. I loved competing, and it played a great role in shaping me into the man I am today. That being said, I realized that of all the areas I wanted to now grow in life, Jiu Jitsu competition was not the most efficient means of doing so. Competing forced me to grow in many ways that I so desperately needed in my 20s, but now as I sit at the ripe, old age of 29, I am very much aware of the new areas in which I need to grow, and competition would not serve this aim. My new "competing" will be more dedicated toward the service of others, and communicating my beliefs on a grander scale.

I got the message, and it was beautiful. I have since hung up the phone. If a new call comes in with a new message, I will surely pick up the phone again. For now, however, competition has served its purpose in my life, and it's time to focus on new challenges that will lead to my becoming who I desire to be.

Thought Exercise

The Battle of Two Wolves

One night sitting around a campfire, an old Cherokee Indian told his grandson about a battle that goes on inside each of us.

"My boy," the old man said, "the battle is between two wolves.

One is evil. It is fear, anger, guilt, arrogance, and ego.

The other is good. It is love, compassion, service, joy, and gratitude."

The grandson meditated on this deeply, and then asked, "Which wolf wins?"

The old man directed his gaze from the fire into his grandson's eyes and replied simply, "The one you feed."

Which wolf are you feeding, and with what does it feast upon?

Part IV - Putting Down the Ax

"Philosophers have hitherto only interpreted the world in various ways; the point is to change it."
- Karl Marx

The Real Reason To Earn A Black Belt

"Become a millionaire not for the million dollars, but for what it will make of you to achieve it."-Jim Rohn

I have been given the rare opportunity to teach Jiu Jitsu for a living. This is a privilege for which I wake up grateful every day, and a responsibility that I hold dearly. I understand how rare it is to be employed through a labor you genuinely love, and one which can be used as a vehicle for positive change in the lives of others. Even rarer still, I am often reminded of the quality of Jiu Jitsu I have learned, and the opportunity to have learned it. Nearly seven years ago, while working as a grounds keeper before becoming a strength and conditioning coach, a friend suggested that I try learning Jiu Jitsu at the school right down the road from my house, and it wasn't until some enlightening years later that I realized how fortunate I was that the school was led by Ricardo Almeida.

Fast forward to today, and now I spend the majority of my time practicing or teaching this beautiful art. As an instructor, my goal has always been to use Jiu Jitsu as a vehicle to help our students achieve their goals, whatever the case may be. I have yet to find a better vehicle for growth, and the moment I do I will certainly pursue it with the rivaled fervor that I approached Jiu Jitsu. Until that day comes, however, I can think of no more worthwhile aim than pursuing mastery in this craft while transcending one's own limitations.

I have been fortunate to know many successful people. Many of whom, most outside my immediate area will never hear their names. As an aside, I think these are the people that are changing the world. Not the politicians or public figures, but the heroes among each and every community who silently serve its greatest good. I have often said that I didn't think the world needed a Messiah, just a few thousand good men and women spread across the globe with the shared aim of service, with their circles of influences neatly connecting.

Of all the successful men and women I have met in my travels, there have been few, if any, who have directed my path as much as one of my instructors, Professor Brian Walter. Through unparalleled technique, competency, and an ability to move toward simplicity, as both an instructor and a student he has always been something at which to aspire. He has been instrumental in my learning all aspects of this martial art-- from uke, to student, to instructor. Beyond his incalculable influence on my ability to perform Jiu Jitsu, his greatest gift in my life has been observing his leadership. A man whose impressive words pale in comparison to the example he sets through action, he has silently brought together a community that so many call home. Of all the lessons I have learned from this man, the most pressing in my mind is that which he taught me in a passing conversation.

I asked him what his goal was for his students. What purpose did he wish Jiu Jitsu to serve in their lives, and how do we most efficiently get them there? Through a wonderful Socratic dialogue led by a man who has probably never read Socrates, I came to see that our student's goals are vast, but can all be met in the same way.

He simply stated the goal is to bring each student from white belt to black belt, and then he told me why. Let's look at the most common goals of our students, and see if achieving black belt will help them achieve their aim.

If the student's goal is to lose weight, will achieving black belt reach this aim? Yes.
If the student's goal is to become more confident, will achieving black belt reach this aim? Yes.
If the student's goal is to learn how to defend themselves, will achieving black belt reach this aim? Yes.

And so it went. Every possible goal of the student would be met by bringing them from white to black. This was the "what" that facilitated their "why." As an instructor, the goal of having all of my students achieve black belt had always been an implicit aim. Now, it is time to make it explicit. Whatever the student's goal, why ever they are here, helping them achieve technical mastery of this craft and the lifestyle which ensues, will bring them to where they want to go. In a world so full of the intangible, I officially had a quantifiable measuring stick with which to measure the success of my students.

But isn't this an obvious goal of the instructor?

I am reminded of the old Zen parable:

"At first, I saw mountains as mountains and rivers as rivers. Then, I saw mountains were not mountains and rivers were not rivers. Finally, I see mountains again as mountains, and rivers again as rivers."

Life is not without lessons!

This is why I feel so strongly that every student of Jiu Jitsu should pursue becoming a black belt. Go to bed early. Stay up late. Whatever it takes. Just keep going.

By becoming a black belt, you will become whatever it is you wanted to be in the first place, and Jiu Jitsu will have served its aim.

Fellowship

"Try to enjoy the great festival of life with other men."-
Epictetus

In a modern world with so many conflicting ideologies, we find ourselves generally on one side of the fence. The secular world ridicules the superstitions of the religious with the seeming lack of empirical validity backing their claims. The secularists cite reason and proof over belief. The religious community believes the claim of the secular world to be science fiction, and their refusal of scripture a dogma of the lack of acknowledgment of the beauty of creation and its creator. Far too common, we derive a sense of self from our beliefs, and we vehemently oppose all which contradicts our beliefs, and their subsets.

Regardless of the validity of the claims purported by the non-believer and believer alike, the religious community has excelled greatly in the one area that the secular world cannot seem to create, fellowship. This, in my mind, is something the religious community has done an amazing job at fostering, as their sense of togetherness, belonging, and understanding within their sect, their exclusive inclusivity, is something that the outside world has neglected to a detrimental effect. The secular world often finds its constituents disenfranchised and solitary as it has spent a great deal of time debating the religious community while failing to build a true community of its own.

Fellowship is one of the most fundamental needs of the human being. American Psychologist Abraham Maslow, father of the popularized "Maslow's Hierarchy of Needs," recognized the importance of fellowship as he placed it in the middle of his now famous hierarchy.

Sandwiching the need of fellowship we start at the most basic of needs, Maslow described the necessity of air, food, water, shelter as the starting point for our existence within the realm of the physiological. Continue up the hierarchy, our next stop is the fundamental need for safety in terms of personal and financial security, and general health and well-being.

Above the need of love and belonging (fellowship), we find the needs of esteem and self-actualization. For humans have the need to feel both respected by their peers, but more importantly respected by themselves, and deemed valuable. With this esteem comes the process of self-actualization in reaching our highest potential. As Maslow put it, "What a man can be, he must be."

It is worth noting that the need for love and belonging comes smack dab in the middle between the lower basic needs of the human experience, and the highest forms of self-actualization. Fellowship is the bridge toward the heights of human experience. It is in community where we find our very selves. The religious community has recognized this fact, and has created houses of worship and extended families in which we recognize ourselves to be a part of something greater than ourselves. We find togetherness, wholeness, and a unity that appears increasingly hard to forge in modern times.

It is fellowship, this most fundamental need on our way toward achieving our highest expression of the human experience, which Jiu Jitsu provides. Across the world Jiu Jitsu has taken favor as the martial art of choice, and this is undoubtedly a product of the nature of the art. Jiu Jitsu is intimate in a way unlike any other. Bodily contact is a prerequisite, and the sheer volume and degree of physical contact (and its accompanied Oxytocin) forge bonds that everyday life simply cannot. Our projected walls of personal space are shattered by its practice as we find both physical and emotional union on the mats.

A Jiu Jitsu academy is a place where men, women, and children congregate from all walks of life, to work toward a common goal of pursuing mastery in an art which transcends into all aspects of their existence. We seek to understand Jiu Jitsu as a vehicle to understand ourselves. We have different explicit goals, from getting in shape, learning self-defense or competition, but tacitly we all seek mastery of ourselves. A pursuit of the utmost importance, but rarely articulated in modern society, we recognize this desire in ourselves and our fellow teammates, and it is this shared pursuit that connects us.

The chaos of the day is washed away, and we are cleansed of the stresses of modern life when we come together in the academy. We find fellowship, we pursue a better understanding of ourselves and others, and we serve one another to whatever extent our opportunities allow. One simply needs to scroll through their social media feed to see the community with which Jiu Jitsu practitioners identify. Forty-something accountants post about arm bars, not tax laws. College kids post videos of the latest competitions, not beer pong.

Jiu Jitsu provides a place of fellowship that, unfortunately, our society has largely failed to create. Yes, we in my homeland are American, but we rarely derive a sense of self (unless personally involved in the military) from America. On a greater scale, we are human, but we rarely recognize our shared experience with the 7 billion others comprising our species. In large part, we feel isolated from our fellow man. Jiu Jitsu transcends this isolation. This art acts as a magnet as it attracts like-minded individuals toward a common goal.

Training Jiu Jitsu will make you stronger. Training Jiu Jitsu will give you the ability to defend yourself. Training Jiu Jitsu will help you lose weight.

But training Jiu Jitsu will make you a part of a community, something larger than yourself, and often this is the most important.

It is worth remembering that toward the end of Maslow's life, he criticized his own interpretation of our human needs as he felt he had missed the most crucial aspect of the human experience, self-transcendence. He later believed that the self only truly becomes actualized when it is given to a calling higher than itself, to the inward spiritual experience and the outward altruistic and service-based experience.

This is the opportunity the fellowship of Jiu Jitsu affords us. To reach our highest potential of self, and then to offer that self to another.

Jiu Jitsu Is A Microcosm Of Your Life

"As long as you live, keep learning how to live."-
Seneca

Jiu Jitsu has incalculable benefits, and not the least of
which is the way it breeds self-awareness. The best
indicator of a man's philosophy is not what he reads or
says, but the way in which he lives his life, the way in
which he acts. Jiu Jitsu is the perfect lens for
introspection and to determine who one really is.
However you train Jiu Jitsu, I have no doubts that this
is the way in which you live your life.

I firmly believe that life will continually try to teach
you the same lesson, with increasing pain, until you
heed the call. Sooner or later, we eventually get the
message and we stop or start doing whatever activity
needs to be done to rectify this problem. These lessons
manifest themselves in various forms from
relationships, business, health, etc. Though they are
expressed through different mediums, they are always
of the same function. Many of these potential lessons
go unnoticed as we suffer our entire lives from various
ills that lie in our blind spot as we fail to connect the
dots. Jiu Jitsu shines the light on many of these ideas if
only we take the time to look.

Consider the problems a Jiu Jitsu practitioner might
face:

Making the same mistake repeatedly without correction

Rushing through techniques

Investing in the outcome (a belt) and not the process (who we become)

Closed-minded during learning

Consider the types of ways in which people train:

Anger, Egoic

Kind, Gentle

Flowing and Effortless

Forceful and Rigid

Erratic movement

Purposeful movement

Jiu Jitsu is a microcosm for your life. Whatever mistakes you are making on the mat, you are undoubtedly making them in life. The same holds true for what we do well. Any positive virtues that present themselves on the mat, will surely present themselves in every day life. Whether good or bad, Jiu Jitsu is the perfect yardstick with which to measure who you are as a person. If you make the same mistakes over and over in grappling, you are doing this in your relationships or at work. If you train in a calm and purposeful way, you can be sure you act similarly in all other endeavors. Consider the way we view training partners. There are those who we love training with, and those we avoid at all costs. Odds are the same holds true for that individual off the mats.

Jiu Jitsu can be a source of total transparency such as a mirror, but it takes a conscious choice to see what it has to say. Take a hard, honest look at your training. What do you do well? What mistakes do you make consistently? How do you train? How would you like to be able to train?

Ask yourself these questions, and use Jiu Jitsu as the vehicle to create these changes in your person. The way you perform Jiu Jitsu will always tell you who you are and what tendencies you have. You just have to be open enough to listen.

Friendships

"Of all the means which wisdom acquires to ensure happiness throughout the whole of life, by far the most important is friendship." -Epicurus

Jiu Jitsu forges friendships in a way I've never known. Being involved in an art as intimate as this, where bodily connection is a must, the common cultural boundaries of personal space are broken. You will never see more hugs, high fives, and physical expressions of love than on the mats. Ultimately, this proves to be one of the most fulfilling aspects of our pursuit of mastery. Along the way, we learn to love others as we love ourselves.

We see it in every locker room across America. When a group of people share in an activity, they bond together in a way that is not possible in everyday life. The harder the activity happens to be, the deeper and more meaningful the relationships will become. This is a product of empathy. Human beings on the whole are empathic creatures, and are inherently well adapted to recognize another's plight, and to feel their pain. There is no better example of this than our booming movie industry. We so often want to get lost in the story, and emotionally invested in the characters, but this is only made possible by our unique ability to put ourselves in someone else's shoes.

When two people share in a particularly challenging activity, they are immediately brought together. They each understand what the other is going through. They recognize the personal sacrifice it takes to accomplish the other's aim, because they share the same desires. Empathy bonds us in a way no other virtue can. When I think of how much of my life I have dedicated to Jiu Jitsu, all of the countless hours of training, watching film, tournaments won and lost, injuries, early Friday nights, and the sheer effort that I have put forth, and I recognize that the man sitting across that mat from me has done the same, How can I not love him? Relationships formed through Jiu Jitsu are deeply rooted in respect for one another, and this is often not the case in matters of modern society.

Consider the trust that two training partners have. A choke is literally taking someone to the point of death, and then releasing him. When two individuals train, there is a tacit understanding that no matter to what degree the training escalates, we will protect each other and do no harm to one another. This is beautiful beyond words. We put our health and our lives in the hands of our training partners, and they do the same. This gives us a small (very small) glimpse of what the friendships in the military must be like. These are deep, meaningful relationships that can only be forged through sacrifice, trust, and mutual preservation. When I think of my own training partners, I consider the fact that I have probably trained with my dear friend Max Bohanon more than any other. We started training around the same time, we had similar dedication and expectations for ourselves, and we received our black belts together. Max is a

2x IBJJF world champion, but this pales in comparison to the type of person he is, and I am lucky to know him. At the time of this writing, we have been training together for 7 years, with a pace and fervor that is not made possible with many others, and we have never once harmed each other. Not once. Considering the nature of the sport, this is an amazing accomplishment that can only lead to a relationship of trust and admiration.

My professor, Ricardo Almeida, often jokes that he is only friends with people who practice Jiu Jitsu. There is more to this than a comical anecdote. If you are reading this book, Jiu Jitsu (or whatever martial art you practice) is a large part of your life, and surely occupies a great deal of your time, energy, and attention. It makes perfect sense that we would pursue relationships with those who have had a similar experience, and can relate to our struggle.

Truthfully, friendships are simply our loving another because we understand them. I believe if we had the opportunity to understand every human being alive today, we would love every one of them. The more shared history and experiences that we can have with another, the greater our understanding of them and the greater our love for them. Through Jiu Jitsu I have developed many of the most meaningful relationships in my life, and if that were the only benefit of my practice, Jiu Jitsu would still be the best endeavor I have ever undertaken.

As Chris McCandless, the lead of the book and film *Into the Wild* realized at the end of his life,

"Happiness is only real when shared."

Service To Others

"Remember this. Hold on to this. This is the only perfection there is, the perfection of helping others. This is the only thing we can do that has any lasting meaning. This is why we're here. To make each other feel safe."- Andre Agassi

Throughout my writing over the years, I have repeatedly expressed what I believe to be the best use of one's life. Life is so unlikely, so rare and beautiful an opportunity it is to live, we must be on constant guard to ensure that our actions are worthy of the life it takes to perform them. Through my lens, there are largely only three endeavors I deem worthy of my life:

Mastering myself, service to others, and appreciating nature.

Though this book is not the appropriate medium through which to express my love for nature, I would like to leave this topic with one thought. In ancient Athens around 400 B.C., Plato theorized what is now known as the "Theory of Forms." I strongly recommend the study of this concept, but for the time a simple explanation will suffice. Essentially, there is a highest reality of the essence of all things in the immaterial world, and it is within our material world that these ideas are expressed through various physical forms. He suggested that we believe things to be beautiful because they are a representation of that ideal form, and more specifically, because we recognize that they possess a virtue we ourselves lack. For me, this is the purpose nature serves. My time in the woods is time spent with a tutor on how to live. Nature reminds me of calm simplicity. Nature is purposeful and deliberate in her actions, but does not hurry. I spend time in the woods because it is these virtues I wish to learn from the woods.

Now, back to the first two worthy endeavors, mastery and service.

A common theme in many of the major religions and spiritual teachings is the idea of the removal of the self. Essentially, ascension to a higher metaphysical reality is a movement from me to we. In a sense, the mastering of yourself is largely in a way of removing that very self, and turning your focus toward the outside world, becoming outer-directed rather than inner. A movement from duality to non-dual. Two-ness to one-ness. I would be remiss had we devoted an entire book to personal mastery while leaving out the ultimate reason for doing so. Keeping with the aforementioned philosophy of beginning with the end in mind, we must remember that the end of personal mastery is service to others. This is the highest good that so many of the revered great thinkers of the past have taught.

The Stoic Seneca knew this well, as late in life while away from Rome he wrote, "I have withdrawn not only from men, but from affairs, especially from my own affairs; I am working for later generations, writing down some ideas that may be of assistance to them."

In my own life, I have always viewed personal mastery as simply a medium through which I become capable of providing more service toward my fellow man. I grow because it makes my experience more enjoyable, but more importantly this growth gives me the better opportunity to positively influence the lives of others. I devote a great deal of my life to reading the great works of philosophy because I know that it is the newfound perspective they bring that makes me a better friend, son, and teacher. Being part of the whole, as I grow so does that which contains me.

In my future home life, I know that the effort I put forth today will translate to a better relationship with my future wife and my future children. When I choose to spend time with Aldous Huxley over Sportscenter, I do so knowing that this is directly improving the family I will someday have. I have always found that effort is most easily produced when performed for the benefit of something external to ourselves.

I remember clearly six years ago, when my dear friend Peter McHugh, now wildly successful school owner and entrepreneur, was preparing for his first mixed martial arts fight. We would go for late night runs together, after a full day of training, and despite physical torpidity, I have never run that fast for that distance in my life. Always staying a few paces in front of him, constantly pushing our pace, this was only made possible because I did not run for myself, I ran for my friend. Life is easier lived when lived for others.

I spent a great deal of my early twenties amid existential frustration. My constant companions of Sisyphus and the existentialists gave me great perspective in formulating meaning for my life, and I boiled it down to the three simple genres above: Love of yourself, Love of others, and Love of nature. It is worth noting, however, that only one of these continues on after you are gone. In some way or another, we all seek to have influence that lasts beyond our very selves. Though mastering ourselves and loving nature are two of the highest activities in the present moment, it is only the service of others that leaves ripples in the world after we have parted.

The beautiful truth about service is that we are afforded countless opportunities to be its vehicle. Every interaction with another is an opportunity to serve. From simply letting someone into your lane in traffic, to holding a door, to a kind smile. This is all service. I am humbled by this simple truth. We are given the opportunity to express the most meaningful use of our lives every time we interact with another sentient being. Each moment we have the choice to express the highest ideal of our being. This is fortune.

We must strive to become more daily. We must honestly assess our weaknesses and overcome them.

We must work toward the highest possible version of ourselves. This is a worthy use of our time, but it is only when we do so with the ultimate aim of service to our fellow man that we really connect with something greater than ourselves. To contribute to the world in a positive way, this is the gift of life.

It is a gift we must receive sincerely.

Thought Exercise

The Story of Two Monks

On a cool spring morning, two monks are walking along a riverbed on their way back to their village. They come across a beautiful young woman standing at the water's edge, hopeful of crossing but the water is rushing too fast and there is no bridge in sight.

Without hesitation, the older monk introduces himself, lifts her off her feet, and carries her across the river. After making their goodbyes, both monks continue on their trip back home.

Used to walking in meditative silence, after a few hours the younger monk can no longer take it.

"Sir, what did you do!? We monks are not meant to interact with females, especially one so beautiful and tempting. It is against our oath!" the young monk cried.

"My dear friend," the wise, old monk replied calmly, "I left the girl back at the river. Are you still carrying her?"

What do you carry, whether it be a belief, world view, relationship, or material possession, which no longer serves you?

Epilogue

Jiu Jitsu Cannot Be The End

I love Jiu Jitsu. Of all the worldly activities, it is undoubtedly my favorite. The way I feel while training must be the way the monks feel while meditating. A complete removal of self occurs and only the highest reality of my expression comes forth. Jiu Jitsu has helped me grow in ways I never knew possible, and has brought me to an understanding of myself and this place that I had never thought could be attained.

I have spent the last seven years of my life, offering up my intellect, time, and emotion in the pursuit of understanding this art, and these were efforts not spent in vain. I have become someone that I had not intended on becoming, I have understood things I didn't know were capable of my understanding. I have seen far by seeing through the lens of Jiu Jitsu. I have exchanged a great deal of physical health for these insights, and these were trades worth making. My efforts were worth the return. I have sacrificed much in the name of this craft. Not for trophies or belts or prestige. For these fall away like dust. I pursued this art so fervently because it was not actually Jiu Jitsu I pursued. It was myself.

I wanted to get to the most essential aspect of my being, and look around for a while. I wanted to explore what I am in my most basic self. I wanted to chip away at all of the nonsense I have acquired through my twenty-nine years on this earth. I wanted to find truth. Thoreau went to the woods. I went to the mats. Jiu Jitsu has peeled the veil of daily life, and has shown me what lies beyond the curtain. We willingly accept the chains that circumstance forces upon us, and we grow to find comfort in them. We attach various fetters of day-to-day living to our being, and we do so with a smile. We accept these constraints for they come in the way of comfort. We accept conformity for it appears the path of least resistance. We strive toward the middle, and we run from ourselves.

Jiu Jitsu has helped me see that this is but one mode of life. One way of viewing the world, and we needn't accept it as an absolute simply because it remains so prevalent. Jiu Jitsu has shown me that we are not confined to the lot which we inherit. We are not bound to these fetters eternally. They are temporal. We can transcend them should we sincerely choose to. Sincere effort is in fact the rarest virtue among man. We are pushed into roles, and we play them well. We find tranquility in docility. We accept what the fates have given us, and we believe ourselves incapable of change.

This is nonsense. We are free to shape the lens in which we view the world. We are free to decide what we value. We are free to reject the values of our environment. We are free to live the life we have imagined, not the life imagined for us. Jiu Jitsu has shown me this, but we mustn't get caught midstream.

Jiu Jitsu is the means, not the end. We mustn't stop here. Jiu Jitsu is the vehicle which affords us the opportunity to transcend our limitations, but we mustn't stop at Jiu Jitsu. We must seek more. We must become more. We must strive for a higher ideal.

Jiu Jitsu is but one interpretation of the divine ground. It is the menu, not the meal. We must use Jiu Jitsu, and the lessons it teaches us, in every area of life that is not Jiu Jitsu. The point of meditating is not to learn to sit quietly in a room. The point is to live that way in the world. The same holds true with our practice of Jiu Jitsu. All of the virtues, paradigm shifts, and adaptations that we exercise in our grappling, must continue on to the rest of your existence. They are not meant to end on the mat. That is the beginning. The genesis. You mustn't be content to be a great grappler. After all, this is simply a game. It is a beautiful, primal, highly cognitively complex game. But it is a game. We must remember that games are played for fun, and for what they make of us to play them. Jiu Jitsu is not the end. It's a means toward a higher realization of your relationship with yourself, and your relationship to your life.

We must keep going with what we have learned. Recall the words of Alan Watts quoted in *Competition*. Referring to the use of psychedelic drugs, but he could have just as easily been talking about Jiu Jitsu, the full quote reads:

"Psychedelic experience is only a glimpse of genuine

mystical insight, but a glimpse which can be matured and deepened by the various ways of meditation in which drugs are no longer necessary or useful. If you get the message, hang up the phone. For psychedelic drugs are simply instruments, like microscopes, telescopes, and telephones. The biologist does not sit with eye permanently glued to the microscope, he goes away and works on what he has seen..."

We must walk away from the mat, and work on what we have seen. We must translate our newfound understanding of the art to a newfound understanding of ourselves. If Jiu Jitsu does not make you a better father, son, mother, daughter, wife or husband, you are missing the point. If Jiu Jitsu does not leave you viewing strangers in a kinder light, you are missing the point. If you are not better equipped to deal with the vicissitudes of life due to your training, then you are not really training.

We call it training. Not because we are training for Jiu Jitsu. We are training for life.

We must use this vehicle for a higher calling within ourselves. Not simply to get better at playing a game, but to get better at living. What higher aim exists than this? Purposeful practice is designed to yield progress not in the task at hand, but in ourselves.

Jiu Jitsu is meant to serve us, not the other way around. It is meant to make you more of whatever it is you already are. It is meant to separate the wheat from the chaff. It is meant to bring to conscious attention all that once went unseen. It is meant to make you more loving. It is meant to make you more wise, but less certain. It is meant to make us humble, yet supremely confident. It is meant to remind us of our frailty while simultaneously making us feel invincible.

It is meant to give us the tools for how to live, not how to fight. It is meant to remind us that we have only scratched the potential of who we are as human beings. It is meant to remind us that Jiu Jitsu is the vehicle. Not the road.

The Only Answer Worth Knowing

Seven short years ago
I began a lover's quarrel with Jiu Jitsu
As my intentions waned to and fro
I had no idea what this journey would amount to.

I competed and fought
I tore ligaments from finger to knee
The greatest lesson this journey has taught
Is I have the control to decide who I'll be.

I at once began to learn how to fight
to be able to subdue my fellow man
It wasn't until I let go of physical might
that I learned all that Jiu Jitsu can.

For it wasn't armbars and sweeps
that would shape the man I would someday become
You see the greatest benefit that I have reaped
is this simple rule of thumb.

Jiu Jitsu will make of you
more than you originally sought
And you must see clearly all the way through
That is was only ever yourself you fought.

Dominion over others is a menial task
and one of which I no longer desire
It is the mastery of self which is of the highest caste
and the service to others that our being requires.

Trophies feel good for a little while
and the dopamine flows from likes on Facebook
but it is only virtues I seek to compile
and turning inward and having a look.

Master the Berimbolo and Judo throwing
and learn to pass the guard through and through
But always remember the only answer worth knowing
Is are you the man Jiu Jitsu sought to make you?

- C. Matakas

Notes